The Teaching Puzzle

The Teaching Puzzle: Your Guide to Social and Emotional Learning

CENTRE FOR
EMOTIONAL HEALTH

First published in the United Kingdom in 2013 by

Family Links
Units 2 & 3 Fenchurch Court
Bobby Fryer Close
Oxford OX4 6ZN

www.centreforemotionalhealth.org.uk

Family Links is a registered charity 1062514.

First edition 2013
Second edition 2016
Third edition 2017

A CIP catalogue record for this book is available from the British Library.

ISBN 978-0-9544709-2-0

Written by Julian Wilkinson, Annette Mountford, Gail Allan, Nick Haisman-Smith and Bea Stevenson

2nd edition direction and project coordination by Bea Stevenson

Cartoons by Val Saunders

Design by Cat Davis - madebycat.co.uk

Printed by L.E.G.O. S.p.A

The Centre for Emotional Health is a national charity dedicated to creating an emotionally healthy, resilient and responsible society. The Centre for Emotional Health encompasses Family Links, Emotional Health at School (formerly known as The Nurturing Schools Network) and Emotional Health at Work.

The Teaching Puzzle is for all trainee teachers and staff working in schools.

The Teaching Puzzle

- Nurturing ourselves
- Creating an Emotionally Healthy Environment
- Thinking about Feelings and Behaviour
- Use of Praise and Guidance
- How to Manage and Deal with Difficult Feelings
- Ages and Stages and the effects of labelling
- Personal Power, Self-esteem and Choices and consequences
- Continuing our Professional Journey
- Effective Circle Time
- Working Effectively with Adults

Nurturing the social and emotional health and wellbeing of children and young people in our schools is essential if we are to provide them with the kind of education that they need and deserve. Improved social and emotional health and wellbeing is, in and of itself, an incredibly important outcome in education – yet we also know that it is associated with a wide range of other positive outcomes including academic achievement, physical and mental health, and employability.

The Teaching Puzzle book, and the accompanying Classroom Handbooks, set out a practical vision for how schools can be emotionally healthy so that everyone can aspire, flourish and achieve.

This book brings together some of the latest educational research to tackle some complex issues – including the use of effective praise, how to guide without criticising, and understanding and managing distressed or challenging behaviour. I do hope you enjoy exploring this book and that taking some of the strategies into your teaching practice is a positive and nurturing experience for you and the children in your classes.

Nick Haisman-Smith

Nick Haisman-Smith, Chief Executive

Contents

Introduction

Chapter 1:
Nurturing ourselves

Chapter 2:
Creating an Emotionally Healthy Environment

Chapter 3:
Thinking about Feelings and Behaviour

Chapter 4:
Use of Praise and Guiding without Criticising

Chapter 5:
Personal Power, Self-esteem and Choices and Consequences

Chapter 6:
Managing and Dealing with Difficult Feelings

Chapter 7:
Ages and Stages and the Effects of Labelling

Chapter 8:
Effective Circle Time

Chapter 9:
Working Effectively with Adults

Chapter 10:
Continuing our Professional Journey

Resources:

What's the book about and who is it for?

Welcome to *The Teaching Puzzle*: the definitive practical guide to understanding and managing the emotional atmosphere in your classroom, school and community. If you have picked up this book, you'll already be aware that working in a school – whatever your role – is one of the most rewarding, as well as challenging and demanding jobs there is. We have written this book to support all staff in the school community with a range of ideas and strategies – some of the puzzle pieces – to help your work be as effective and enjoyable as possible. Putting the pieces together will promote emotional wellbeing, relationship skills and positive interactions between adults and children alike within the school community.

"It's great to find a source of new strategies and ideas for my school."

The ideas in this book are based on the Nurturing Programme, a whole-school and community model which provides children, young people and adults with a combination of cognitive (thinking-based), affective (feelings-based) and behavioural strategies to help them get the best out of family, school and community life.

We know you will already have strategies for supporting your children but we hope that this will add strategies to your toolbox.

The book is designed for school staff working with 3-11 year olds and can also be used to support transition to Key Stage 3.

The Nurturing Programme

CENTRE FOR EMOTIONAL HEALTH

The Centre for Emotional Health is a national charity dedicated to creating an emotionally healthy, resilient and responsible society. The Centre for Emotional Health encompasses Family Links, Emotional Health at School (formerly known as The Nurturing Schools Network) and Emotional Health at Work. We have 20 years' experience developing, delivering and evaluating emotional health programmes across the UK.

Through our education programmes, we help children and staff in schools and universities develop good social and emotional health that supports their learning.

Our aim is to build an active community of schools, universities, teachers and parents who are committed to promoting emotional health and wellbeing, to enable everyone to aspire, flourish and achieve.

Our range of training courses and resources provide school staff with ideas and strategies to establish emotional health as the bedrock for an inspiring learning environment. They underpin a school community whose ethos encourages peer group co-operation and social responsibility, as well as building relationships with and supporting parents to engage fully in their child's learning and the school.

The Four Constructs

American child psychologist Dr Stephen J Bavolek developed the Nurturing Programme in the 1970s. Bavolek researched dysfunctional and abusive family interactions; he identified four destructive parental behaviour patterns and developed the Nurturing Programme to counter these, known as The Four Constructs.

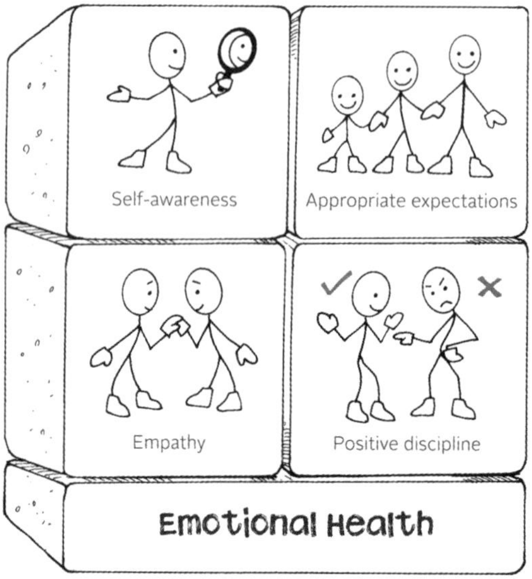

The Four Constructs

Self awareness

being aware of our own needs and feelings and taking responsibility for them. Meeting our own needs helps us to be more nurturing to others. Building our self-esteem helps us to aspire and achieve.

Appropriate expectations

understanding that children grow up in different ways: physically, intellectually, socially and emotionally. As adults working with children we need to match our expectations to what each child can reasonably manage. If we expect too much of them the child is likely to feel frustrated and inadequate, and give up trying. If we expect too little they feel disempowered, fail to aspire and give up.

Positive discipline

children need to learn what behaviour is okay at school and what is not. Positive discipline focuses on praise, rewards, giving choices and consequences, negotiating and sharing responsibility. There are also fair consequences for poor behaviour. Negative discipline uses punishment and fear, is stressful for everyone and is not effective in the long-term.

Empathy

the cornerstone of the Nurturing Programme and the ability to tune into someone else's feelings and see things from their emotional point of view. An empathic response to children's moods makes our relationship with them happier and closer. Children who are treated with empathy and respect will learn to be empathic and respectful towards other people.

Why is this book needed?

Children learn best when they are feeling safe, appreciated, understood and involved. School staff work best when they feel positive, unstressed and supported by other staff. This book provides the puzzle pieces to help you be the teacher or staff member you want to be in a way that is both sustainable and enjoyable. We hope you will feel inspired, confident and re-energised!

We know that the benefits of this approach can help your school succeed.

Here are some extracts from Ofsted reports on schools using the Nurturing Programme:

"There are very good procedures to support pupils personally and to help them develop as individuals. At the heart of this is the school's total commitment to the Family Links Nurturing Programme. All members of staff use the same methods of praise and discipline; they all expect the same high standards of behaviour."

"The school's commitment to promoting education in values through its Family Links programme is an example of very good practice."

"All staff, including catering and site staff, have received detailed training for the Family Links Nurturing Programme and they set good role models for pupils in every aspect of school life. The teaching was characterised by very good relationships between staff and pupils, very effective use of circle time techniques and good opportunities to reflect on pupils' own worth and how to work and play together successfully."

How is the book organised?

It is divided into chapters, many of which are introduced to the children during Circle Time over the course of a 10-week term, and the topics explored by parents and carers through its partner book, *The Parenting Puzzle*.

Each chapter contains:

- **Key messages** of the chapter 
- **Did you know...?** thought bubbles offering extra ideas to reflect on or further reading
- **A classroom window** showing you a possible scenario, along with a backstory, which helps us to think about how a child's behaviour might be affecting their school life
- **Staff member** reflections to support key messages
- **The Staffroom** at the end of each chapter, helping you identify with the questions and comments raised.
- **Checklists** to help summarise the chapter
- **Questions** for you to consider
- There are also **workbreaks** - many of which coincide with themes looked at through the book. Workbreaks are quick activities that will change the energy of a class if they are getting tired or distracted, restless or over-excited.

Bringing social and emotional learning into your schools

The Teaching Puzzle is designed to help school staff with practical and pedagogical approaches for creating and maintaining a positive classroom climate. When children learn in this kind of nurturing environment, we know that they will feel safe, included, able to engage fully with learning, and take healthy risks.

We also know that as teachers we can do more, through the curriculum, to help children develop the resilience and skills that will enable them to aspire, flourish and achieve.

This is why we have developed four age-appropriate Classroom Handbooks. These handbooks contain Circle Time lesson plans and games which provide your class with the knowledge and skills to become emotionally resilient and socially skilled individuals.

Our approach to Circle Time is a vehicle for developing children's emotional literacy in the following ways:

- Improving their speaking and listening skills
- Extending their powers of concentration
- Enhancing their relationships with each other
- Helping them consider not only how they themselves - *but also how others* - feel
- Enabling them to express their views and feelings
- Encouraging them to value and respect each other's differences

- Developing their confidence and self-esteem
- Supporting them as they learn to be kind, not only to each other but also to themselves
- Establishing a sense of community
- Having fun

Classroom Handbooks

The handbooks are available in the following age ranges:

Early Years Foundation Stage Handbook

(EYFS: 3-5 year olds)

Key Stage 1 Classroom Handbook

(Years 1 & 2: 5-7 year olds

Key Stage 2 Classroom Handbook

(Years 3, 4, 5 & 6: 7-11 year olds)

Transition Handbook

(Years 6 & 7: 10-12 year olds)

The Classroom Handbooks and *The Teaching Puzzle* complement each other and are best used together. There are a range of other resources, including the The Nurturing Game, with which to create an environment which inspires and sustains positive attitudes to help your children aspire, flourish and achieve.

The Teaching Puzzle cast

As you read through the book you will be meeting all *The Teaching Puzzle* characters. We hope that they will help you to identify with some of the day-to-day scenarios that can happen at school and some of the more personal feelings of staff and parents. They will also show you some of our ideas in action!

Year 1:

Mr George

Billy

Billy's dad

Year 2:

Ms Johnson

Harvey

Harvey's dad

Year 3:

Mrs Evans

Jake

Jake's mum

Year 4:

Miss Davis

Maya

Maya's mum

Year 6:

Mrs Khan

Lauren

Headteacher:
Mrs Wilson

The Staffroom

"I'm really looking forward to getting started and trying out lots of ideas!"

"I am determined to make this school a positive learning environment."

"I'm not sure that I need this as my classroom works fine as it is."

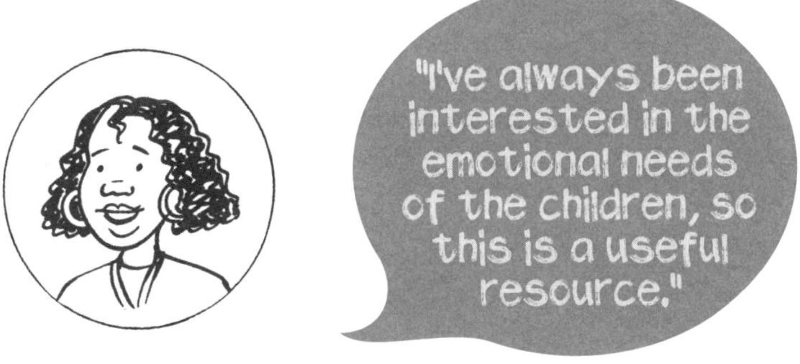

"I've always been interested in the emotional needs of the children, so this is a useful resource."

Chapter 1: Nurturing ourselves

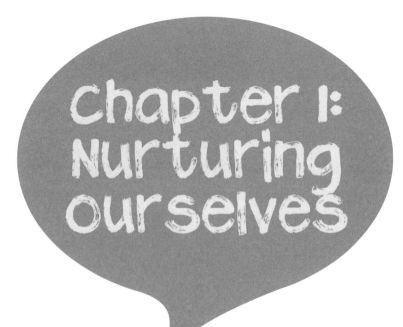

Being a role model

As an influential adult in their lives, you are always modelling for the children. Think about what behaviours you are modelling. Are you calm in tricky situations; do you have a positive attitude to learning yourself?

Taking the time to plan out your classroom and modelling respect for the things in it can be extremely powerful. Also, carefully sharing how you are feeling with children (such as expressing tiredness or frustration) can allow children to identify their own feelings and think about coping strategies.

> "I've come to a frightening conclusion that I am the decisive element in the classroom. It's my personal approach that creates the climate. It's my daily mood that makes the weather. As a teacher, I possess a tremendous power to make a child's life miserable or joyous."[1]

Getting the best out of life

How I can get the best out of work and home life and take responsibility for my own wellbeing

Working with children can be one of the most demanding jobs there is. To enjoy it, we need to think about our own emotional health and mental wellbeing. Thinking about your own also shows the children how much you value their emotional health.

> "You've got to be in a good place within yourself if you're going to try and get the best out of children."
>
> Francis Murphy, Deputy Head

1. *Haim Ginnott, Teacher and Child: A book for parents and teachers, Prentice Hall 1993*

During the school year, staff give out a great deal of themselves. Working in a school is a very intense job and if you're having an 'off' day, you can't just sit quietly in the corner and drink tea. It's a job that makes great demands on you and, because you are involved in shaping the lives of children, and communicating your thoughts and concerns to their parents, it's also a very responsible job.

"This is definitely an important topic for me to think about. My staff can feel very stressed and tired, especially in the run up to Christmas."

Your energy and input into your class or school has a direct impact on the group of children you are working with. This can be very exhausting. It's important to think about how you can make time for yourself and fulfil your own needs as well as those of the children you work with. No-one feels 100% positive, cheerful and motivated 365 days a year! However, you can do things to make sure that you feel as enthused as you possibly can.

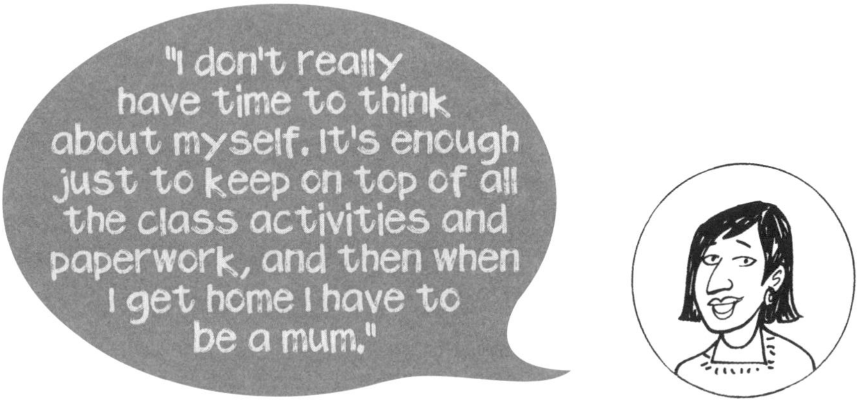

"I don't really have time to think about myself. It's enough just to keep on top of all the class activities and paperwork, and then when I get home I have to be a mum."

our social and emotional health

Our emotional health is governed by how well we know ourselves and can handle our feelings. This goes for adults as well as children. It's often referred to as emotional intelligence.

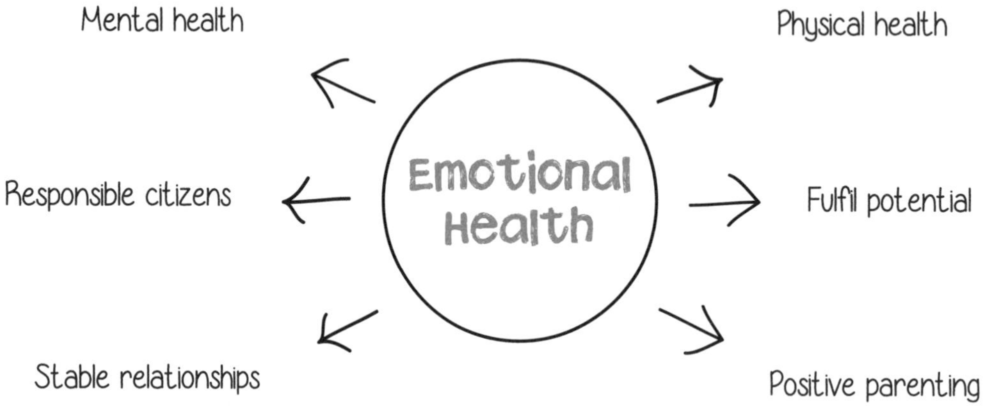

The impact of an emotionally healthy school on learning and behaviour cannot be overestimated. Research tells us that looking after our emotional health is a key component for reaching our potential and making the most out of life's opportunities. Non-cognitive skills are associated with positive outcomes for young people, according to a large body of research.[2] Factors such as self-control and school engagement are correlated with academic outcomes, financial stability in adulthood, and reduced crime.

Children with emotional problems are much more likely to do poorly at school and twice as likely as other children to have marked difficulties in reading, spelling and mathematics (Green et al., 2005). Almost 50% of young people with fewer than five GCSEs graded A* to C said they "always" or "often" feel down or depressed compared with 30% of young people who are more qualified (Prince's Trust, 2012).

2. See www.educationendowmentfoundation.org.uk/uploads/pdf/Non-cognitive_skills_exec_summary.pdf

It can be helpful to think of social and emotional health as comprised of five different but related concepts. Under each heading you will find some questions to ask yourself and some ideas that might help.

1. Knowing our emotions
2. Managing our emotions
3. Motivating ourselves
4. Recognising emotions in others
5. Handling relationships

1. Knowing our emotions

This is all about self-awareness and recognising a feeling as it happens. It's the foundation of emotional health.

- How well are you able to monitor your emotional state from moment to moment?
- How did you feel when you came into school this morning?
- How do you feel now?

It's important to recognise what emotional state you are in. This can help to explain your behaviour. Emotionally literate people are able to monitor or observe their emotions however turbulent they may feel at the time.

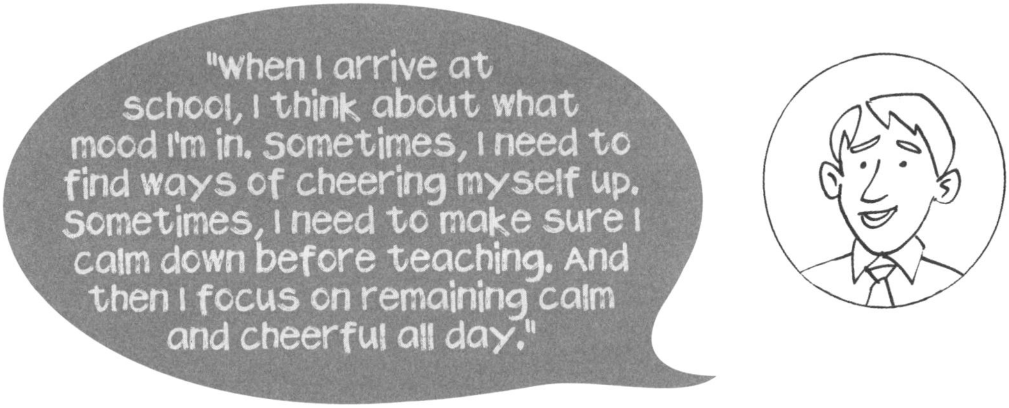

"When I arrive at school, I think about what mood I'm in. Sometimes, I need to find ways of cheering myself up. Sometimes, I need to make sure I calm down before teaching. And then I focus on remaining calm and cheerful all day."

2. Managing our emotions

The ability to handle our feelings builds on our awareness of them. We need to be on good terms with all our feelings. We need ways to soothe ourselves when anxious, calm ourselves when angry, and contain ourselves when agitated.

- **Do you have a strategy for calming down if you feel stressed or panicky?**
- **Are there ways that you can lift your spirits when you feel unhappy or low?**
- **How do you handle situations in which you feel angry?**

It's important to acknowledge feelings of anger and sadness. They have their place in everyday life and give us important signals about the situations we encounter. So how do we manage these feelings? It's a question of balance: every feeling has its value and significance; it is the ratio of positive to negative emotions that determines our emotional wellbeing. The aim is to be in charge of our emotions rather than a helpless slave to them.

"If I am angry about a certain situation, I never make a decision in the heat of the moment that I might regret. I take a deep breath and say that I will think about things and give my children or my colleagues my response later."

3. Motivating ourselves

If we can marshal our emotions to help us identify our goals and reach them we become productive and effective. When we are enthusiastic and confident, we are more likely to be motivated and resilient. When we are distressed by difficult feelings, we can't think straight. When we are simply indifferent, our motivation is low.

- **How easy do you find it to think clearly and make decisions?**
- **Do you feel that on most days you manage to get everything done to the best of your ability?**
- **How motivated are you to perform well at work?**

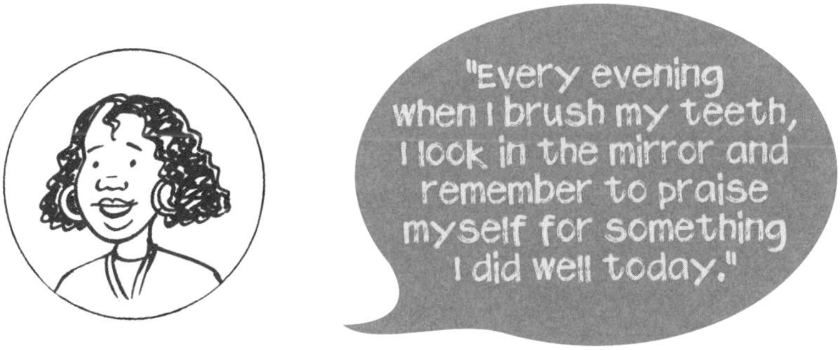

"Every evening when I brush my teeth, I look in the mirror and remember to praise myself for something I did well today."

4. Recognising emotions in others

Empathy is the ability to be sensitively aware of the emotions of others and is one of the most important people skills. It's also a vital ingredient in developing rewarding relationships. What people say in words doesn't always reveal their emotional state. We need to sense how they are feeling by being open to other signs, such as tone of voice, facial expression and body language. These are all indicators of emotion.

- **Think of a good friend or child in your class. How can you tell when a good friend or child is feeling sad?**
- **When you are talking to someone, are you aware of other emotional signals apart from the words they are saying?**
- **Are you understanding of colleagues who have difficult emotions?**

"Every time my friend Eve feels sad about her mum, she finds it difficult to chat. I give her hand a squeeze to show that I know how she is feeling."

5. Handling relationships

Handling relationships is a bit of a balancing act! We need skill to understand and support the emotions of others while also managing and effectively expressing our own. Emotions are contagious: we transmit our moods and catch those of others. Emotionally skilled people are open and positive. We can trust them with our feelings, and we feel good when we are with them. Learning these skills ourselves enhances all our relationships. Ask yourself:

- Do you consider yourself to be open and honest with your friends and colleagues?
- Do you think you express yourself well and get your point of view across effectively, more often than not?
- Who among your friends and colleagues do you consider to be the most emotionally skillful? Why is this so?

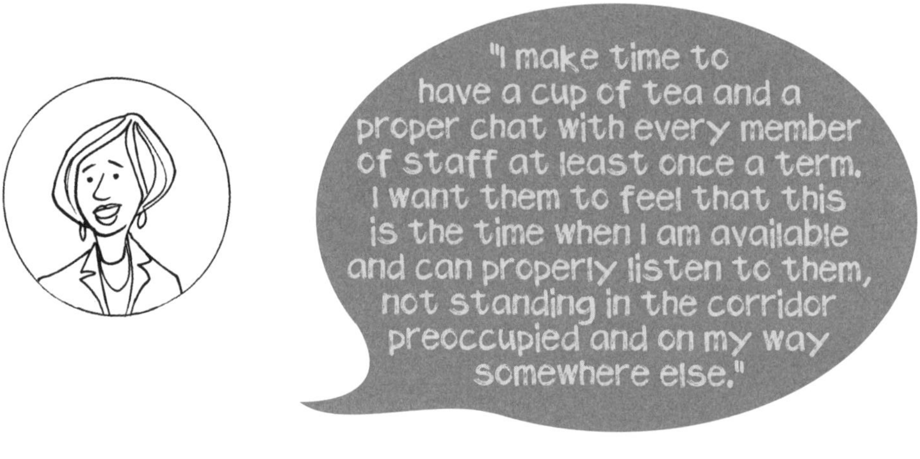

"I make time to have a cup of tea and a proper chat with every member of staff at least once a term. I want them to feel that this is the time when I am available and can properly listen to them, not standing in the corridor preoccupied and on my way somewhere else."

Nurturing ourselves

The idea of taking the time to think about looking after ourselves might feel a bit uncomfortable at first. Sometimes we are encouraged to feel that thinking about ourselves is selfish or wasteful; it may give rise to feelings of guilt and discomfort. It might help to think about it as a vital tool that will help you be the person you want to be. It can be useful to think of this as role-modelling self-respect. If we boost our reserves, and make sure that we have a strong and resilient emotional system, we are much better equipped to be a great teacher.

You can even buy a set of Nurturing Ourselves postcards from our website: centreforemotionalhealth.org.uk – remind yourself and encourage a friend by posting one!

Did you know... ?

On aeroplanes, if you have to use oxygen masks you are instructed to put on your own mask before helping children. Caregivers that nurture themselves are better equipped to nurture others. Burn-out and stress are the result of ignoring the basic needs of the self.

The first step is to take responsibility for our own needs. The Nurturing Programme offers a simple acronym to help us remember these: SPICES. Nurturing ourselves spices up our lives! Have a look at the Nurturing Wheel on the next page.

The Nurturing Wheel

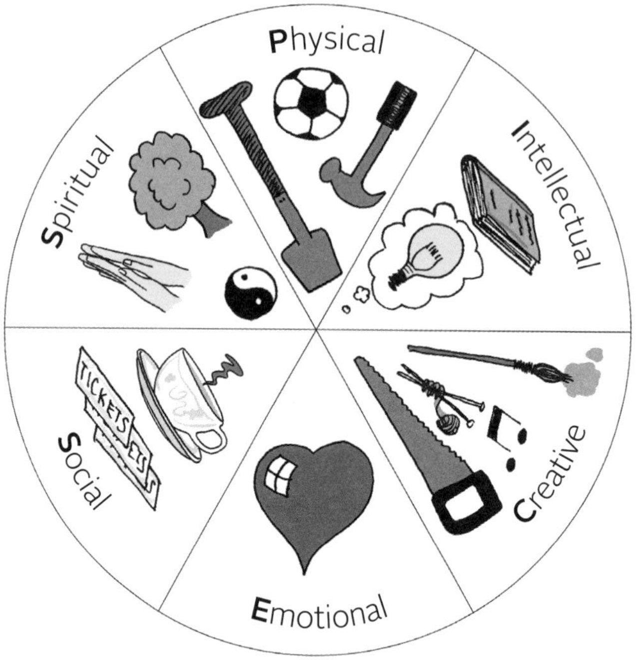

Social needs	friendship, companionship
Spiritual needs	increasing our sensitivity to nature, faith, a sense of awe and wonder
Physical needs	food, sleep, exercise
Intellectual needs	new ideas, thoughts, mental stimulation
Creative needs	making or doing something, expressing ourselves
Emotional needs	loving and being loved, empathy, understanding, laughter

When things don't feel right

It can seem overwhelming to try and change our lives if we feel that things are very wrong and not running smoothly. The patterns of behaviour we have built up are often stubborn and tricky to shift. Change can take time, but think of it as a series of steps with each one taking you in the right direction. Walking with a heavy backpack is tiring and difficult but once we remove some of the load it's far easier to walk in comfort. *The following questions will help you make a start.*

Questions to ask myself:

My environment

- Am I happy with the environment I work in at school?
- Is it well-designed and well-organised?
- Does it make me feel productive as soon as I arrive at work?
- Is my home – or any part of it – a sanctuary or haven?
- Is there somewhere where I can truly relax and shut the door on the rest of the world?

An unhappy home environment can make a difficult day at work much worse.

My boundaries

- How do I set boundaries for myself?
- Do I manage my time well?
- How successfully do I balance work and leisure?
- If I feel exhausted, do I give myself permission to stop?
- Do I sometimes feel that I am overstretched and doing nothing well?
- Do I feel that I can let a colleague know if I am feeling overwhelmed and need them to relieve the burden?

My listening skills

- Do I make time to listen to those I am close to?
- Do people make time to listen to me?
- When I do listen to someone, do I think about my body language?
- Do I make sure that the environment is right when I want someone to listen to me?

Praising myself

- Am I motivated at work?
- Do I feel confident and equipped to do the job?
- Do I have good self-esteem?
- Do I make positive use of my Personal Power?

My labels

- Am I very sensitive to what people think of me?
- Do I continue to act out the labels that I was given as a child?
- Do my beliefs mean that I don't fit in?

Identifying which of the above might apply to you will go a long way in helping to start to change things for the better.

It's the little things that count

If you are feeling stressed and overwhelmed a few simple changes to your daily life can make an enormous difference.

It can be exciting to plan for bigger breaks and periods of relaxation during the school year, such as a holiday, an evening class or a long weekend away, but think too about the smaller, everyday opportunities to focus on yourself and relax. We have made a list of a few here. Of course, different people will favour different activities, as the Nurturing Wheel identifies.

See if you can add some of your own to this list:

Do some exercise, perhaps going to the gym or for a run

Make a cup of tea

Meet up with friends

Walk in nature

Play a sport, individually or as part of a team

Unplug from all electronics - phones, tablets, TVs for a day

If we introduce these moments to de-stress and clear our heads, we will wake up with the energy and drive to make a difference, and not the feeling that we are at the end of our tether.

Think about where each activity fits on the Nurturing Wheel and you will begin to see how you can fulfil each need.

Time for me

This is the place to refresh your memory a bit by looking at the following questions and having a go at some of the challenges. You can always look back at the topics in this chapter if something isn't clear.

How well do you look after yourself?

Write down your ideas as a reminder to build in time for yourself every day.

What I do for myself now

every day	once a week	sometimes

What I'd like to do

every day	once a week	sometimes

What prevents me *(negative thoughts and practical concerns)*

What I can tell myself instead

Letting go

The Nurturing Programme has several relaxation exercises that you can use to help you and your class let go of difficult feelings. One of the most useful is the Hot Air Balloon. You can either do it at home on your own or in the classroom with your class.

If you do plan to use it in the classroom, this exercise is best done with a class who have already explored difficult feelings through Circle Time. Ask the class to sit or lie comfortably with enough distance between them so as not to distract each other. Invite them to close their eyes.

Start to relax by taking several slow, easy breaths... and now begin to picture a brightly coloured hot air balloon, floating just above the ground and ready to lift its basket and drift off into the sky.

When the balloon and the basket are clear in your mind, take any angry, sad or difficult thoughts and feelings and put them in the basket. There's plenty of room in there for them all.

Now picture the balloon slowly lifting off the ground. Gradually it rises up until it is outlined against the clear, blue sky. Keep watching it as it rises into the air, getting higher and higher, until it begins to get smaller and smaller as the breeze carries it away. As it goes, it carries away all your difficult feelings.

Where those old feelings were inside you, imagine a new big, open space that is light, airy and peaceful, and as you watch the balloon drift away, until it is only a speck in the sky and then vanishes, let yourself be filled with the light and space and peace...

For details of other workbreaks and relaxation exercises please refer to pages from 213 in the Resources section. You can also use the Classroom Handbooks and go to www.relaxkids.com.

The Staffroom

"This chapter has been a real eye-opener for me. Helping my staff to remain calm and happy in their jobs and making sure they look after themselves will now be a priority rather than an afterthought."

"I go for a run every morning and I make sure that for half an hour each evening I read something that has nothing to do with school. It's working wonders!"

"In my first year as a teacher, I would start working again as soon as I got home. After a few weeks of that, I couldn't sleep and just lay awake making lists."

"I always use Thursday nights to write my plans for next week's lessons. That way my weekends starts on a Friday."

Chapter 2: Creating an Emotionally Healthy Environment

What's my classroom climate?

How to establish a positive learning environment

The classroom climate is a helpful way to think about the emotions, relationships and dynamics that comprise any learning space. The climate might be warm, positive and productive when children are in a good place emotionally, and when relationships between both adults and children are nurturing and with clear boundaries.

"Every day I want to make my classroom calm and stress-free, but sometimes this is just so difficult to achieve."

Creating a positive working environment within your school can therefore make a huge difference to how children learn. Developing and maintaining this positive classroom climate requires the use of intentional and proactive strategies, alongside thoughtful, more responsive approaches. This chapter will give you the tools you need to do this.

Think of yourself as being the thermostat for your class or school environment.

There is research evidence that improving the classroom climate has a positive impact on student outcomes.[3]

3. 'What Makes Great Teaching Report?' - Sutton Trust Review of the underpinning research – R Coe 2014

Have a look at the following questions and think about how they apply to you.

Questions to ask yourself:

- How do I feel when I begin the day?
- How do the children in my care feel when they begin their day?
- What is the climate in my classroom on a Monday morning? On a Friday afternoon? During a wet breaktime?
- Could I change anything to make the atmosphere calmer and more positive?
- Are there any particular times of day that trigger difficult behaviour?
- Can children tell me when they are sad or frustrated?
- How have we created our classroom agreement?
- How do I use my voice in the classroom?
- Do I ever feel the need to shout to make myself heard?
- How are the children in my class seated?
- Do I listen enough?
- Do children listen to each other?

As you read through this chapter, you may find answers to these questions.

Thinking about boundaries

Setting and maintaining clear and firm boundaries is one of the ways we can establish a positive classroom climate. For some children it will be more of a challenge to keep to boundaries, depending on their experiences at home and in other settings. We have identified four main kinds of boundaries that children and young people may come across:

constricting

If we are constricted and over-controlled, we may become rebellious and uncooperative, or go to the other extreme and become timid and submissive, waiting to be told what to do and reluctant to try things for fear of making mistakes.

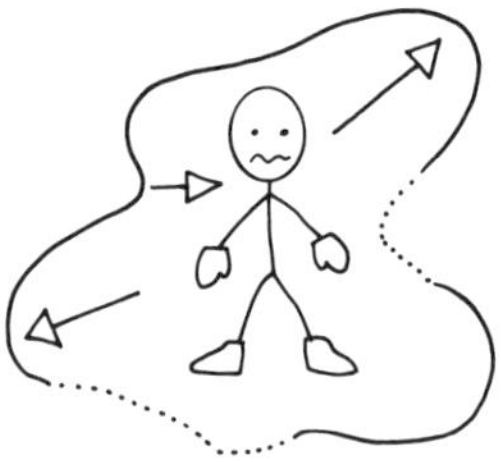

inconsistent

With inconsistent boundaries we feel confused and insecure, and also learn to be manipulative. If the adults around us aren't clear about what they expect of us, we can't learn what behaviour is okay. A lot of difficult behaviour can be traced back to this.

Absent

Too much freedom can be as scary as not having enough. If there are no boundaries, we may feel that nobody cares about us and may behave in extreme, and sometimes dangerous, ways in an attempt to get someone to take charge.

clear, consistent

Fair, firm, kind and consistent boundaries help us to feel secure, safe to explore within the limits and to test them; this leads to confidence, an ability to try things without taking foolish risks, and respect for others. These are helpful boundaries: consistency, particularly when we are young, is important.

Which of these boundaries do you identify with? *The ones that feel familiar may be those you knew as a child, or have seen other adults use.*

All of us can be **inconsistent** at times. Here is an example of inconsistency:

How do you think the class might feel in this situation?

What do they learn from Ms Johnson?

By having clear guidelines from the start, children understand what behaviour is appropriate. Of course it's a challenge to promote consistency between different staff, since we all have our own professional style.

Classroom agreements

It's easier to stick to consistent boundaries if we have clear, fair agreements for everyone in school. In the next section we look in detail at how to set up a system that helps everyone feel safe and comfortable, and supports efforts to co-operate with the agreed rules.

Making a classroom agreement is a key part of creating a positive climate. We believe that the best way to do this is to build an agreement together with the children in your class or school. This allows you to share ownership of the rules with the children, as part of a process which is explained in Week 1 in all of the Classroom Handbooks and which provides an early lesson in citizenship.

We know that children are more likely to stick to classroom agreements if they have had a say in developing them. When they emerge from a discussion about what helps children to learn and what stops them from learning, the agreements will have real meaning for the children, who will feel more accountable if they break them. The agreements should be designed to meet the needs of the children.
It is much more helpful to them in the long-term if they learn co-operation through understanding and self-discipline rather than compliance.

clear, fair
agreements
help us all
feel safe

DOs and DON'Ts agreements

One way to do this is to introduce the idea of DOs and DON'Ts agreements which can be used as classroom or school agreements. In either case it's a good idea to have a staff discussion first to ensure consistency. Discussing appropriate consequences for each of the classroom agreements with the children as part of a circle time can also be very powerful as it maintains their sense of responsibility for their choices.

These help everyone to know not only what they should be doing, but also to be clear about what they shouldn't be doing.

It helps when we keep the statements simple and very specific ('be good' would be too general) and don't make the list too long, (especially for younger children); four rules are quite enough. Visual rules (especially of 'DOs') can really benefit some children. Perhaps you could use photos of different children in the class modelling DO behaviours.

DOs	DON'Ts
Do raise your hand if you want to say something.	**Don't** shout out.
Do talk to the person next to you about work.	**Don't** talk about other things or distract others.
Do listen respectfully to others.	**Don't** make fun of others or laugh at them.

A fun way of bringing this exercise to life, for Key Stage 1 and 2 classes, is to put a large smiley face (DOs) at one end of the classroom, and a sad face (DON'Ts) on the other. Then you, the teacher, read out the classroom behaviours and the children run to the side they think the behaviour would correspond to. For example, 'kicking' should be matched with the sad face and 'clearing the art table' with the smiley face.

Agreements quiz

The *Key Stage 2 Classroom Handbook* uses an Agreements Quiz with Year 6 classes in Circle Time.

Give each child a copy of the Agreements Quiz *(see below) and invite them to fill it in by asking different classmates one question each. Return to the circle and conclude that this activity may have helped people notice things they haven't noticed before, such as unspoken agreements at home.*

To see the full session plan, see Year 6 Week 1 of the *Key Stage 2 Classroom Handbook* (you can order it from our website, centreforemotionalhealth.org.uk).

Are pets allowed in your bedroom?	Do you have to eat everything on your plate?	Can you watch TV whenever you like?
Can people in your family borrow things without asking?	Do you help with shopping?	If a grownup is cross with you at home, what happens?
Who does most of the cooking in your family?	Whose job is it to tidy up your toys?	When someone in your family feels sad, is it okay to cry?
Are you allowed to play with a ball indoors?	Do you have a fixed bedtime?	Ask a question of your own

Classroom window

The backstory

Ms Johnson has put a lot of time and effort into planning this Circle Time. She has been talking to the children about how they would like to feel as a class, and what helps them learn and enjoy school. The children are now ready to contribute to the classroom agreement.

What you could do to help:

Having a consistent whole-school approach to setting rules is a great way to help children keep to boundaries. At the beginning of each term, try to discuss this together as a staff and then each class will go through the same process. Everyone will start by thinking about how they would like to feel in the class and what might help them learn. This activity is the starting point for setting up classroom and school agreements. You will already have many other ways to include children and adults in decisions about school life: a school council, suggestion box for parents, good ideas board in the staffroom, etc.

Steps for Successful use of Classroom Agreements

1. Refer to the agreements regularly and ask children to consider whether or not they are sticking to them
2. Encourage the class to remember that the reason for the agreements is "to have good feelings that help us to learn"
3. Involve children in changing or adding to the classroom agreements during the course of the year if necessary
4. Try linking the agreements to your reward system - particularly a collaborative one (We will be looking at reward systems in Chapter 3)
5. Display the classroom agreements on the wall for everyone to see and ask the class to write their names around the border (or with younger children use handprints)
6. There are lots more ideas in Classroom Handbooks. For more information and to buy one, go to centreforemotionalhealth.org.uk

Suggestions

In Chapter 9 we will look at the importance of consistency across the whole school and how headteachers can encourage this. If senior management teams work together to agree a shared set of boundaries and expectations, all the adults will have a clear understanding of the ethos and values of the school. It's very useful if the senior management team allows staff to feel that they have contributed to – and have a sense of ownership of – what frames the school and sets the agenda. Children who experience shifting boundaries with different adults in school are often confused about what is expected of them.

Many schools will also share ownership of the physical environment of the classroom and the school. Encourage children and colleagues to make suggestions.

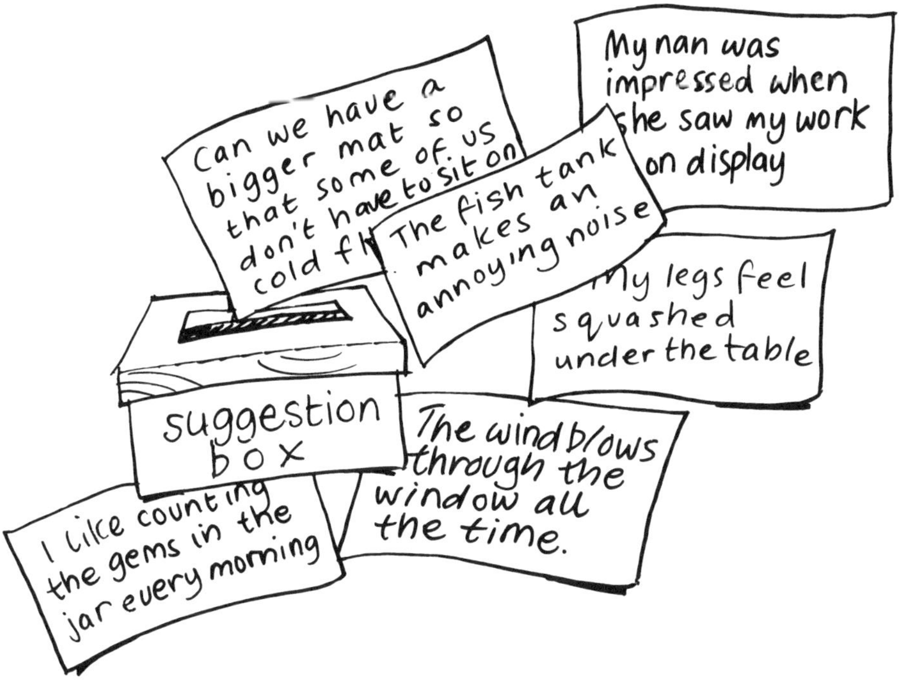

This will really help children to feel that they too have a responsibility towards their environment, that they can make choices about it and that their ideas will be listened to. New ideas can help all of us feel refreshed, motivated and full of energy. Now have a look at this second classroom window to reflect some more on this.

Classroom window

The backstory

Harvey is very hot because his mother insists that he puts on full school uniform every morning. He doesn't have any summer shorts and he doesn't realise that he can take his sweater off. He is also seated at the back of the room which is often stuffy and airless. He is worried that he will be in trouble if he takes the sweater off.

What you could do to help

This might be a good time to revisit your classroom agreement. Asking Harvey and the other children about how they would like to feel in the class may produce some useful and shared new ideas.

You can see that Harvey is uncomfortable and needs help to re-focus on the lesson. You can suggest that as soon as he comes into school on a hot day he leaves his jumper on his peg until it's time to go home. Make sure he has access to water if he needs it and think about placing him near a window to work.

Measuring the emotional climate

It may be helpful to think about the emotional climate in your class or school. This can be too hot or too cold. We will be talking more about helpful and difficult feelings in Chapter 6, but a simple way of measuring the emotional climate in your classroom is to create a mood indicator. There are lots of different ways to do this. One way is to use the traffic light colours of red, amber and green to work out how each child might be feeling. Involve the class in thinking about mood words associated with the three traffic light colours.

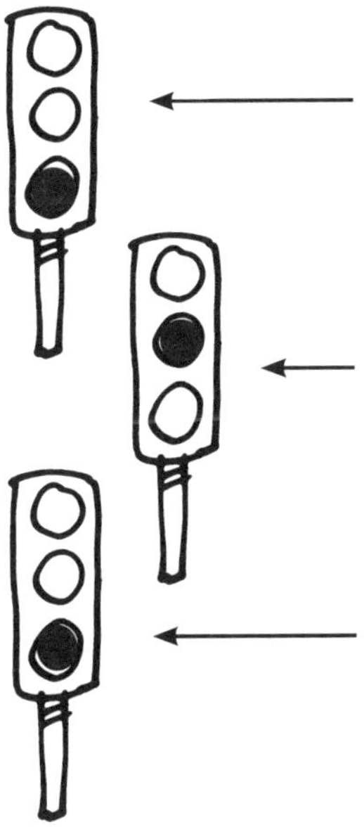

Red – feelings that may stop us from doing things

sad scared sick angry lonely

Amber – feelings that may slow us down

shy tired confused uncertain hurt

Green – feelings that move us forward and help us to get the best out of the school day

happy energetic confident safe proud

Children can tell you how they are feeling simply by pointing at one of the colours on the traffic light. It's an easy way for a child to signal unhappiness without talking about it and it will alert you to any problems. This doesn't mean that children should always be in the green zone and never in the red zone. Sometimes, such as when experiencing a bereavement, it may be very appropriate to be in the red zone.

My Dad shouted at me this morning for losing my shoes and now I feel CROSS!

What could help Billy return to the green zone?

It's also a quick way of checking in with yourself. If you've slept through your alarm clock or battled through traffic before getting into work you might find yourself climbing into the red.

you are the thermostat in the classroom so it's really helpful to know how to turn the heat down!

One of the reasons why it's important to measure the emotional climate in your classrooms is to create the best possible learning environment for the children. If you or the children come in stressed and upset, this has a direct impact on teaching and learning.

Mr George will have a difficult start to the day if he arrives at school late and agitated. So what can we do to help ourselves and others lower the emotional temperature?
See the next page for some ideas.

Transitions

It's important to ensure calm, quick and effective transitions during the day, when clear expectations are given. These can include coming from home into school, transitions between lessons, lunch and break, assemblies and the end of the day.

Here are some ideas for you to try to help children transition throughout the day.

Attention grabbers

Attention grabbers take the tension out of the moment when you need to quieten everyone down and bring them together. It means you don't have to use a raised voice to get attention. It might involve a prop that makes a sound like a jingling bell, or it could be a simple instruction to the class to clap back to you when you clap, or to raise one arm as soon as they see you do so. Ideally use a prop that is both visual and auditory. *If you consistently use the same attention grabber, the children will get used to it and respond automatically.*

Fidget bag

If a child is very restless, having something to fiddle or play with might channel some of their physical energy and allow them to listen more easily to what is going on in the class.

Shoeboxes One idea for children is to have shoeboxes of different colours – red, amber and green (see page 49 for what each colour represents) – where they can put a note or a picture in the appropriate box to describe what troubled or excited them before they got to school or when they come in from the playground. This is the first step in the process of letting troublesome feelings go (which we deal with in more detail in Chapter 6: Managing and Dealing with Difficult Feelings). Anything in the red box will be picked up by the teacher later who will offer to talk to them about it.

Transitions can also be 'created' throughout the day. Keep an eye on the emotional climate of your class throughout the day and react appropriately by providing a change, such as a workbreak or by increasing the pace of an activity.

Music can also be used, both to create a calming atmosphere first thing in the morning, as well as a cue for tidying up, or bringing children to the carpet.

workbreaks to help with transitions

Further ideas for workbreaks for transition can be found in the Resources section from page 213. These ideas can be introduced at Circle Time as the ideal opportunity to reflect on feelings and how we handle them.

These are quick activities that will change the energy of a class if they are getting tired and distracted or need energising or calming down. You can introduce them into the day when you need something to bring everyone back together again. Here are a few examples from the Classroom Handbooks to help you to keep the energy in your classroom positive and conducive to learning:

Workbreaks for changing the pace and increasing concentration

Pass the Ball

The class sits in a circle with outstretched legs. Place a ball on the legs of one member of the group, who then tips the ball gently onto their neighbour's legs. The aim is to get the ball back to the first player without it touching it the floor.

Colour Stamp

The caller calls out a colour and the children stamp around the room to touch something of that colour. The game may be played until a number of colours have been called out.

Workbreak for using up energy

Popcorn

Everyone in the class bounces up and down. If someone bumps (gently!) into someone else, they link arms and bounce together – sticking together like sticky popcorn. The pairs then become fours and the fours become eights, until the whole group is stuck together and bouncing in unison.

Workbreaks for enabling a calm transition from home to school or breaktime to class time

Music Relaxation

The class sits on chairs in a circle, or on the floor, preferably with hands resting in laps and eyes closed or looking downwards. Whilst playing quiet, soothing music encourage the children to focus quietly on their breathing, gradually making it soft and slow.

Pass the Bell

The class stands (or sits) in a circle and passes a small handbell from person to person, focusing on not letting it ring.

All of these ideas and more can be introduced at Circle Time, as the ideal opportunity for reflecting on feelings and how we handle them. Circle Time offers the chance to rehearse for reality. We all know from personal experience that the best time to think about feelings and behaviour is before or after an explosion, rather than in the middle of it when we can't think straight.

Did you know...?

Laughter helps us learn!

If we laugh, it increases oxygen to the brain via the diaphragm hitting the vagus nerve. This leads to feelings of increased contentment, concentration and learning. So a relaxed, laughing child is more likely to concentrate better and learn more.

Shankoff, J. & Meisels, S. *Handbook of Early Childhood Intervention* Cambridge University Press, 2000

Checklist

for a Socially and Emotionally Healthy Classroom

- [ ] This is the place to refresh your memory a bit by looking at the following questions and having a go at some of the challenges. You can always look back at the topics in this chapter if something isn't clear.

- [ ] Create a classroom agreement if you haven't already done so; review the list of rules with your class if you have.

- [ ] Using a traffic light or mood thermometer (see page 31), measure the emotional climate in your classroom every day for a week. See if you can work out the triggers that cause it to turn red.

- [ ] Think about a particular child who is displaying signs of anger and unhappiness and then make a list of reasons as to why you think that might be.

- [ ] Draw a classroom plan highlighting areas that might be uncomfortable, noisy or distracting for children.

- [ ] Think of three more ideas of your own that will create positive energy for your class and defuse any tension or stress.

The Staffroom

"We make sure that all the school agreements are displayed so that children, parents and staff understand our expectations."

"A calming workbreak really helps to settle the children after a noisy lunch break."

"I realise some of the boundaries were very inconsistent, and I didn't involve the class enough in creating the classroom rules."

"I like the idea of an attention grabber. I could create one to mark the end of lunch break!"

Chapter 3: Thinking about Feelings and Behaviour

All Feelings are valid

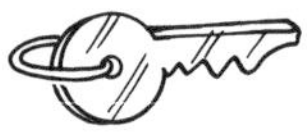

We are emotional beings and as we grow up we experience many different feelings that we need to identify and learn to manage

These feelings are like signposts: they tell us about safety and danger, trust and hurt, love and hate, desire and dislike; we need them all.

To be emotionally literate is to be able to 'read' our feelings and those of other people. If we can learn to accept, manage and healthily express a range of emotions, it will help us live our lives to the full.

It might be helpful to start off by thinking about what can happen when we have feelings that are difficult for us and others.

What we do with difficult feelings

The swirl image in each drawing represents our feelings, and the drawings suggest some of the ways we might react when we have those feelings. Some ways of reacting are helpful and healthy, but others aren't as good for our emotional health.

Acting out

Being overwhelmed by our feelings, often losing control by shouting or resorting to violence

Suppressing

Locking away our feelings, burying them and trying to remove them from our day-to-day consciousness

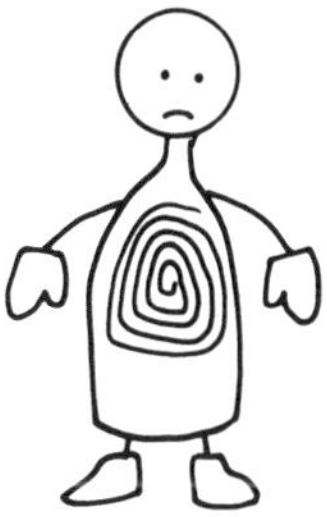

Bottling up

Holding the feelings tightly inside us; we may become so pressurised that we eventually explode

Withdrawing

Hiding away from others; we may feel helpless, even to the point of depression

Dumping

Blaming others for how we feel and trying to hand over responsibility for our feelings to others

How we could cope better with difficult feelings

The five ways of coping with difficult feelings that we have listed so far may make them temporarily go away, but they don't actually solve the problem. Here are some more constructive alternatives that can help us get to grips with what caused the feelings in the first place, and therefore help us make a full recovery.

Reflecting

Accepting our feelings without being overwhelmed by them; we think about them and find ways of resolving them

Expressing

Letting our feelings out, talking about them with others or taking safe action to release them (e.g. crying or doing some physical exercise)

Letting go

When we have fully understood and acknowledged what our feelings mean to us, we can release them

If we have no way of letting difficult feelings go, they can pile up until they're like a huge, heavy sack that we have to drag around with us. This can be hard work and feels awful too!

For further reading try The Huge Bag of Worries *by Virginia Ironside. It's a great way to support children in talking about their feelings.*

As discussed in the first chapter on nurturing ourselves, when working with children it is important you feel able to manage your own emotional health well enough to be available to support children in learning to manage theirs. With our helpful role-modelling, we can encourage them to understand their feelings and express them in safe, responsible ways. Far greater attention is now being paid in education to the need for emotional literacy because of its impact on learning.

Questions to ask yourself:

- Am I able to express my own feelings easily?
- When I was at school, did I hide how I felt?
- Did any feelings get me into trouble as a child?
- Do I make time to listen to the children in my class?
- What feelings might an aggressive or withdrawn child be experiencing?
- Could I use the class mood thermometer to take my own emotional temperature?

"When I was at school I was afraid of making mistakes, but I never showed anyone how anxious I was."

"As a girl I was taught that it wasn't okay to be angry and now I tend to bottle things up."

Encouraging emotional literacy

One of the roles of a teacher is to help children learn how to express themselves. The more words that children have to express their feelings, the less they need to use behaviour to show them. Here are some ideas for words in a Feelings Wall that support you and the children in describing how you are feeling. You may like to add some of your own in the blank boxes at the bottom.

Feelings Wall

sad	*angry*	*afraid*	*calm*	*strong*
jealous	*happy*	*bored*	*excited*	
contented	*misunderstood*	*encouraged*	*fed up*	
capable	*lonely*	*kind*	*tearful*	*generous*
embarrassed	*amused*	*rebellious*	*friendly*	
aggressive	*safe*	*worried*	*comfortable*	
hurt	*valued*	*frustrated*	*interested*	*shy*
confident	*inadequate*	*determined*		

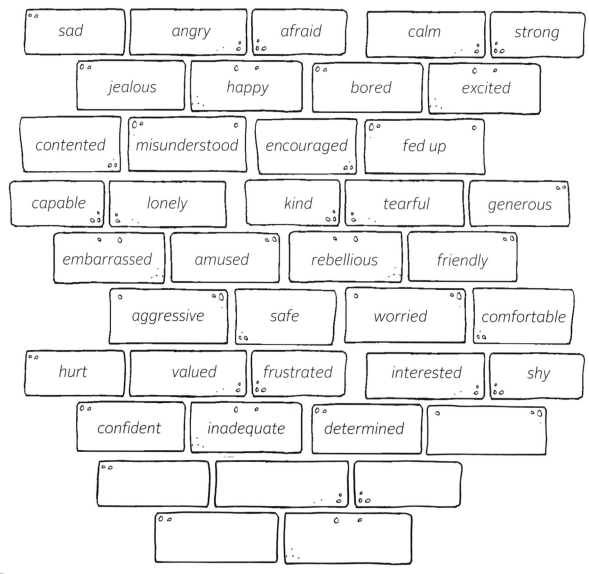

Another classroom idea is to have a Feelings Quiz involving bricks from the Feelings Wall. Ask the children to complete the sentence on each brick.

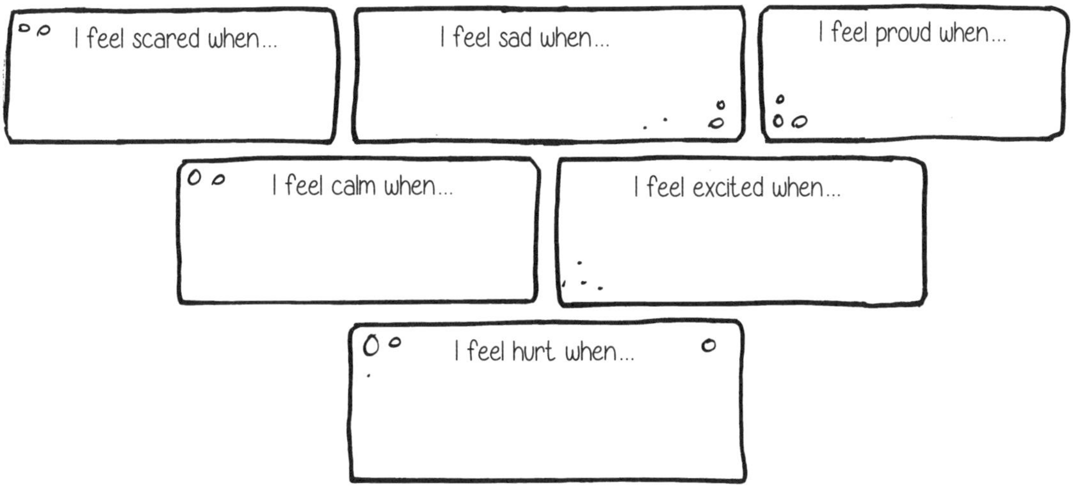

You could also ask parents to add a comment to the Feelings Wall as a way of involving them in classroom activity or even build a Feelings Wall in the school entrance for parents' and carers' contributions.

When a child shows difficult behaviour it's helpful when we can empathise and think about the feelings that might lie behind it. It can be transformational for a child to feel that you've listened to him or her. It also allows you to help a child deal with difficult feelings before they trigger more disruptive behaviour.

We will talk more about good listening skills later in this chapter, but first of all we want to introduce the idea of empathy and its place in the classroom.

What is empathy and why is it important?

Empathy is the cornerstone of all healthy relationships including those between children and adults. It's one of the Four Constructs of the Nurturing Programme (see page 11). These provide the building blocks for confident teaching and constructive relationships in the classroom. We will be exploring all of these Four Constructs throughout the book, beginning in this chapter with empathy. Empathy means tuning into someone else's feelings and understanding their emotional point of view. We don't have to share their feelings, just understand how it is for them. It is very much about being in the moment with them.

Questions to ask yourself

Can you think of a situation when you turned to someone for support and advice, but were left feeling as though they didn't really understand you or listen to what you were saying? or if they just started telling you what you should do about it?

- **How did you feel towards that person?**

Now think of a time when someone responded empathically to you.

- **How did you feel towards them and about your situation?**

Children who are treated with respect and empathy will learn to be empathic towards other people. Depending on their age and stage of development they may not be able to grasp the concept of empathy easily, but seeing an adult role-model using empathy encourages them to identify with the feelings it arouses. Using empathy will also help with behaviour management as it can defuse negative feelings.

Here's an example of a situation that could be handled in two ways:

Unempathic (unhelpful)

Empathic (helpful)

By using empathy, Mrs Khan was able to defuse Lauren's outburst. She then found a time later in the day to talk to Lauren quietly and find out what was wrong, rather than reacting in front of the whole class. Her thoughtful approach ensured that Lauren's frustration did not escalate into bad behaviour.

She could also develop the discussion by helping Lauren to think about how she could better manage her difficult feelings (see Chapter 6). Make time to talk to children who have had tricky moments at school. It can be hugely valuable both to the child and to your relationship with them.

The language of empathy

Sometimes it helps to have a starting point for responding empathically to another person, such as:

"That seems..."

"You seem..."

"I wonder if..."

"That sounds..."

"You sound..."

Now think about the following comments from children.

How would you respond to them?

We have given you a couple of unempathic and empathic responses for the first one. Try to think of some empathic responses for the other comments, using the sentence starters above to guide you.

"It's not fair - I'm never picked for the team!"

Unempathic responses:

"There's no need to make a fuss about it."

"I'm sure you'll get picked next time."

Empathic responses:

"You sound as though you're feeling left out."

"It seems you're feeling upset about how teams get picked."

Have a go at filling in some responses to the following comments, using ideas from the the sentence starters on page 66.

"Nobody would play with me today."

"I'm no good at writing!"

Did you remember to stick with the feelings and not go into fix-it mode?

Steps for Empathy

1. Stop what you're doing
2. Remain calm
3. Give full attention and listen
4. Ensure appropriate body language and facial expression (crouch down at the level of the child if necessary)
5. Find the right time to allow the child to tell their story
6. Try to focus on feelings rather than issues
7. Avoid questioning or advising
8. Avoid over-reacting or fixing

Classroom window

Why is Maya so distracted? Why is she not paying attention to Miss Davis? How could Miss Davis react?

The backstory

Maya is actually a very organised child and the reason she is looking out of the window is because she has left her cardigan draped over the branch of a tree in the playground. The cardigan is new and she is worried that her mother will be cross if she loses it.

What you could do to help:

One way Miss Davis could react is to criticise Maya for not paying attention and make her sit at the front of the class, then later impose a penalty. Another way could be to ask Maya why she needs to keep looking out of the window and wait for the explanation. Then Miss Davis could either send another adult out of the class to retrieve the cardigan, or reassure her.

Did you know...

What teenagers want from their parents?

A study of adolescents revealed they wished that adults would: listen to our point of view, have firm moral/ethical views, feel positive about themselves, know how awkward, confused, inarticulate we can feel, behave as if they like us.

This study [4] of adolescents' views revealed that being listened to was the most important change they wanted in their families. The sample of 1,174 boys and 1,169 girls and their parents revealed that almost 75% of the young people, but only 41% of their parents, considered that children feeling listened to and understood was important.

The Art of Listening

One of the greatest gifts we can give each other is to listen. Really being listened to attentively and kindly encourages trust, honesty and openness between people. It's a great way to boost self-esteem and improve communication in all our relationships, with both adults and children. *It sounds easy and yet it isn't always that easy to do.*

If someone is talking to you, how often do you find yourself being distracted by your own thoughts? Or interrupting to give good advice or talk about something similar that happened to you?

If we can switch off our own agenda, and really switch on to the other person, focusing on what they are saying and tuning in to the feelings behind their words, it makes a world of difference.

4. *'National Family and Parenting Institute Survey of Teenagers' Attitudes to Parenting,' conducted by MORI, Jan/Feb 2000*

Our body language and eye contact also send a message about how well we are listening.

Sometimes it works best just to acknowledge that someone is feeling sad and not to qualify it or fix it. For instance, nothing is going to bring back a pet that has died. Showing that you're sad for the child and that you understand their feelings of loss is enough. The fact that you are listening reinforces empathy.

If you have a large class and cannot give a child your full attention, simply explain that you will find a time to listen later, perhaps during a Circle Time session or at the next available breaktime. That way, the child will not only feel the relief of being understood but also avoid feeling the frustration that can quickly lead to poor behaviour. Which means that you, too, will feel the benefit. Do make sure, though, that you find the time later to give your attention.

The question of discipline

The word 'discipline' is often understood as meaning a harsh, unkind punishment, which can make the idea of positive discipline seem a bit strange at first. In fact, the word has the same origin as the word 'disciple': a follower, someone who is guided. In the Nurturing Programme we think of it in this way: discipline is a system for guiding children, not for punishing them. We return to this in Chapter 4 when we look at Guiding without Criticising.

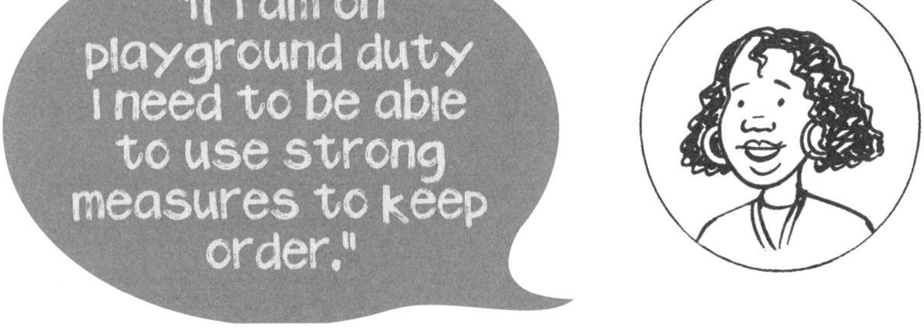

"If I am on playground duty I need to be able to use strong measures to keep order."

We appreciate that you might have thirty or more children in your class, and at least a hundred in the playground, so of course you need discipline to maintain order and calm within the school. What we suggest is that there are two types of discipline – positive and negative – and one works much better than the other.

Positive discipline

Positive discipline is encouraging. It recognises that young children need time to learn what behaviour is OK and what is not, and also that they will make mistakes. It focuses on what they are doing well, rather than what they do wrong. It keeps the adults in charge, while at the same time encouraging children to think and act for themselves in a responsible way. In the first chapter we talked about the need for clear, consistent boundaries. Positive discipline supports these. It spots good behaviour and rewards it, and it uses reasonable penalties in response to unacceptable behaviour.

Negative discipline

Negative discipline focuses on what children are doing wrong. It can be harsh, unfair and inconsistent and forces children to be obedient rather than encouraging them to co-operate. It might teach them what they must not do, but it rarely explains what's right or acknowledges good behaviour. Equally, an over-indulgent and very soft approach to discipline might not be harsh, but it can still be unhelpful. The following cartoons illustrate these two approaches.

Checklist

- [ ] You could use a Feelings Wall as a way to explore feelings in class.

- [ ] Think about each child that you work with in terms of how emotionally literate they are and how you might increase their range of emotional vocabulary.

- [ ] Practise using the language of empathy on friends and family.

- [ ] Practise some really high quality listening: make time to be available to a child, colleague, friend or family member. Practise giving your full attention, with positive and affirming body language and uninterrupted time for them to say whatever they want.

- [ ] There are some great ideas in the Classroom Handbooks for exploring emotional literacy through Circle Time. See centreforemotionalhealth.org.uk for more info.

The Staffroom

"I'm going to organise a couple of sessions for all the staff on empathy and listening skills."

"This has made me very aware that I'm not very good at listening to the children. I'm quick to judge - and I don't always get it right! This has made me think a bit more about how empathic I am."

"I really want to create time to listen more and asking parents and carers to contribute to the Feelings Wall has really interested the class."

"I think I'm learning to be a lot calmer and not raise my voice, but when a child has stepped over the line and really lost it, I'm still not quite sure how to handle that!"

Extra notes on Chapter 3

Chapter 4: Use of Praise and Guiding Without Criticising

Giving praise

Celebrating success through effort

Relevant, purposeful praise can be the magic ingredient in motivating children to learn and increase their sense of possibility. By praise we mean giving positive feedback about the behaviours of others (adults as well as children) as a powerful way of showing that we are pleased, enthusiastic or grateful. It can include:

- Encouragement
- Appreciation
- Positive reinforcement
- Valuing the efforts of others

Praise given about a child's effort to a task supports the child to attribute their achievements to hard work rather than ability and therefore be more accepting of challenge and resilient to failure. Children who have this sense of possibility are less likely to be distracted by anxiety or the fear of failure.[5] As a result they are more likely to co-operate and learn, and have the confidence to try out new tasks.

How do you feel when you receive praise? On the left are some ideas about the emotions you may experience. Put a ring around the ones that you feel and add your own ideas about what the children in your school might feel.

5. 'Good job, you're so smart": The effects of inconsistency of praise type on young children's motivation' Zentall, S. R., & Morris, B. J. (2010) *Journal of Experimental Child Psychology*, 107, 155 – 163.

Positive feedback

The power of positive feedback works for all of us. However, you know the children in your class best and should adapt praise accordingly. We can often underestimate children's ability to recognise when praise isn't genuine.

Praise may be perceived by some to be detrimental to a child's motivation if given too frequently. For some children it may also be a source of embarrassment or a feeling that they are being 'singled out' at the detriment of others. With these children it's important to offer praise in a low-key way. Here are some ideas:

- Praise students as a whole class and stress how an individual child's performance contributes to the success of the class
- Focus on the child's support for another student rather than personal achievement
- Encourage self-assessment and peer feedback

Did you know...

Positive relationships with others and feeling good about ourselves releases natural chemicals (such as serotonin and oxytocin) in the brain that helps concentration. Like plants, humans will struggle in a difficult climate and thrive in a nurturing one.[6]

6. For further reading see Gerdhardt, S 'Why Love Matters' Routledge 2015

Process vs. person praise

Praise for effort rather than ability

Praise for process

You have worked so hard at your painting,
I love the way you've drawn the tree.

Most recent research[7] emphasises the importance of highlighting particular actions rather than abilities. Process Praise, or Praise for Doing focuses on what the child does and in particular their effort. It is therefore earned and conditional. It's a great way to encourage good behaviour choices and pay attention to what we want more of. Being viewed as naturally good at something may stop children finding new strategies or taking risks as they are likely to want to play it safe. Children praised for effort may well recognise that success and value come through hard work, learning new things and development. They're more likely to believe they can grow and understand that learning is hard work; not getting the right answer straight away is okay and part of learning. This is connected to what is known as a 'growth mindset'.

Person praise or praise for being

Another type of praise relates to personal qualities or abilities. This is sometimes called Person Praise or Praise for Being, and depending on how it is used, it can be both helpful and unhelpful in motivating and encouraging children.

Person praise that is specific and avoids labelling the child can be a really useful way to show the qualities we appreciate. For example, we may say to a child that we have noticed how helpful they were today. This type of person praise is still contingent on them behaving in ways we like, so it is still conditional. What all children also need is true Praise for Being: unconditional praise that appreciates and acknowledges them for who they are. We may, for example, tell them how pleased we are to see them or how happy we are that they're in our class.

7. For example: Mueller CM and Dweck CS. 'Praise for intelligence can undermine children's motivation and performance. Journal for Personality and Social Psychology '75(1): 33-52, 1998.

I'm so glad to see you back. We missed you while you were away.
praise for being
praise for doing

This reinforces our unconditional positive regard for them and may be particularly important for children who rarely receive this sort of praise at home.

However, closely linked to this is a second type of Person Praise [8] that has a much less positive effect, and in the long term can lead to the development of a 'fixed' mindset. For example, we might say to a child *"you are really helpful"*, *"you are so kind"*, or *"good boy/girl"*. This unspecific, labelling praise can lead children to believe that their self-worth is contingent on them being *"kind"* or *"helpful"*. It can also lead to a sense that their abilities are unchangeable, making it hard for them to make improvements or tackle challenge or failure. It can lead to the child feeling restricted by the label' they have been given. For example, *"you are so quick at mental maths!"* can prevent them from taking on more difficult tasks and they may see themselves as no longer good at mental maths if next time it takes them longer. See Chapter 7 for more on the effects of labelling.

Have a look at the following statements and decide whether they are giving feedback on the process or the person.

"That's a fantastic painting. You've worked really hard today."

"You have a lovely smile and it cheers everyone up."

"Well done for putting capital letters at the beginning and full stops at the end of every sentence."

"Great presentation! I like the way you're beginning to join your letters."

"You're so quick at mental maths!"

"What a caring person you are!"

"You are so creative with ideas for games in the playground."

"You were very kind to share your crayons with the rest of the table."

"Thank you for stacking the chairs so quickly."

8. *Further reading: Gunderson, E, Gripshover, S, Romero, C, Dweck, C, Goldin-Meadow, S, & Levine, S 2013, 'Parent Praise to 1- to 3-Year-Olds Predicts Children's Motivational Frameworks 5 Years Later', Child Development, 84, 5, pp. 1526-1541, 2013*

What does effective praise look like?

Now that we have identified how praise can be used to support children to feel confident and motivated in their ability to succeed, let's think about how we can give positive feedback to a child.

Unhelpful

Helpful

In the first cartoon Miss Davis offered praise, but it could have been much more effective. Maya was left feeling disappointed and frustrated.

The quality of Miss Davis's praise was clearly very different in the second cartoon. How might this help Maya?

Miss Davis gave her full attention and showed this by picking up on the detail of the headdress. Above all she was sincere. Have a look at the Steps for Giving Praise and Guidance on page 88 for more detail on how to do this well.

Communication when conveying emotion

Communication is a key element in building relationships and conveying information effectively. However, communication is so much more than talking: the actual words that come out of our mouths are only a small fraction of the total communication package. You might think what you have said is quite clear, but a range of factors will affect what the listener hears.

It is well-known that we communicate via verbal and non-verbal methods. Gestures, tone of voice, eye-contact, the way you stand, as well as the words we say are all filtered and interpreted by the listener.

The relationship between non-verbal and verbal communication in the conveyance of emotions, feelings and attitudes, was studied by psychologist Albert Mehrabian. His model identified that non-verbal communication is often more dominant than the actual words you use:

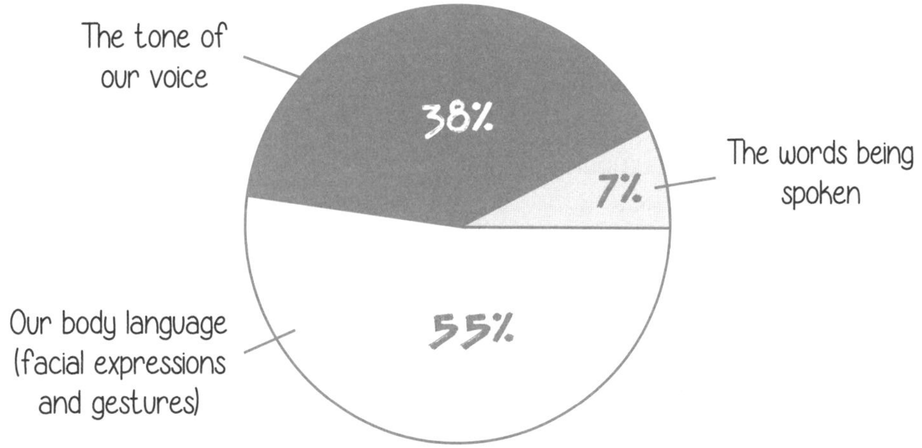

The implication of this when communicating emotions, feelings and attitudes is that the listener will pay more attention to non-verbal cues than the verbal. Mismatches between the different cues may lead to anxiety, confusion or distrust due to conflicting messages.

For example: *A teacher may use praising words towards a child, yet by their non-verbal communication be making it clear that they are distracted and uninterested. This in turn may result in the child feeling unimportant or criticised.*

Guiding without criticising

Take time to consider how a child should be given constructive feedback

Let's begin by thinking about what it can be like when we receive criticism or negative comments. Here are a few examples of how people can feel when they are criticised. Put a ring around the ones you often feel. You can add your own ideas too.

When I am criticised I feel...

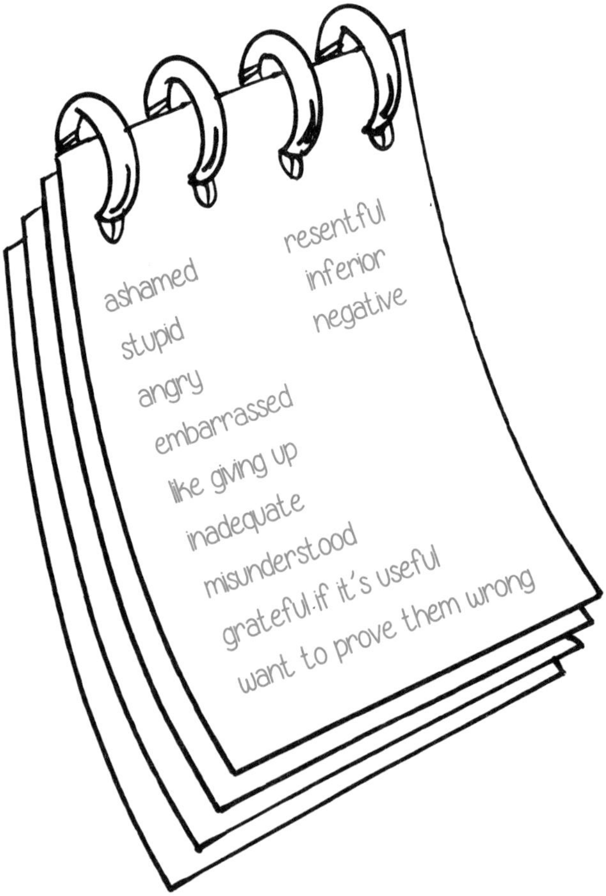

As an adult we may have the ability to rationalise things or consider that comments might be well intentioned but criticism can still be upsetting and hurtful. How might children feel when they are criticised? Do they have similar feelings to the ones that you have identified? For children it is much harder because they put their trust in adults.

While we need to be clear and firm with children about behaviours that need to be improved, it doesn't help to criticise. As we have just discussed in Positive Discipline on page 72, guidance needs to be clear, firm and given in a non-threatening way. Feeling criticised can lead to other difficult feelings as above, and difficult feelings often lead to difficult behaviour.

On this page are some illustrated examples of guiding without criticising.

Unhelpful

Helpful

Unhelpful

Helpful

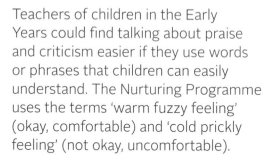

Sometimes the children in my class are just badly behaved. What am I supposed to do then?

When I stay firm, fair and consistent it helps everyone behave better, including me! It helps to think about the feelings behind the behaviour too.

Remember: all behaviour has a reason: it's being driven by feelings.

Teachers of children in the Early Years could find talking about praise and criticism easier if they use words or phrases that children can easily understand. The Nurturing Programme uses the terms 'warm fuzzy feeling' (okay, comfortable) and 'cold prickly feeling' (not okay, uncomfortable).

With older children you can expect to use a wider vocabulary as a stepping stone towards identifying their feelings and expressing them more clearly.

It's always worthwhile to take a moment at the end of the day to think about how often you have praised the children and how often you have said something negative to them.

There will of course be days when you raise your voice or feel snappy. There will also be days when a child cries or is aggressive. It's when this begins to form a pattern that you need to think about what might be going on behind the behaviour.

Have you also thought about how children could support one another through praise and giving feedback? Here is an idea for how different staff members and children can recognise and value one another.

Last week Kate helped me when I was sad.
Kate's House
Ahmed defended another classmate when she was being teased.
Ahmed's House
Today Harvey gave a gentle 'high five' to Harry.
Harvey's House

Did you know... ?

Evidence from around 100 studies shows that 'co-operative learning' - when team members are taught strategies for supporting each other's learning - leads to substantially improved achievements for all participants. The whole team is rewarded for the successful learning of each team member which makes everyone more effective.[9]

9. Slavin, 1996, in Hart et al, 2004

Steps for Giving Praise

1. Give the child all your attention
2. Move so you are near to the child
3. Look pleased and share their pleasure
4. Be specific about what it is that you like
5. Ask the child what they think
6. Seek eye contact
7. Be sincere and show that you mean it
8. Encourage the child to feel proud

Steps for Guidance

1. Find a good time to give the child feedback
2. Be specific about the behaviour or work that you think could be improved and why
3. Compare what the child is doing now with what they have done before
4. Encourage and support further effort
5. Try to focus on complex or challenging tasks

Giving rewards

Having a simple reward system in your class or school helps to motivate children to learn and to behave appropriately. It builds on the feedback you give them, recognises their efforts and gives them clear guidelines for how to achieve. Rewards and class goals all contribute to a more positive learning environment.

For helping a younger child when she was sad.

We have already looked at a number of different ways in which we can give praise and it's also true for rewards. There are all sorts of ways in which children can contribute to the life of the school which don't just involve being good at numeracy and literacy. Sometimes it's easy to slip into the habit of giving rewards only for work and penalties only for behaviour, so it's worth thinking about ways of restoring the balance.

Many schools already have a reward system and your school may well have a Celebration Assembly or something similar once a week, where children's achievements are recognised. We can give rewards for a wide range of behaviour as an incentive to all children and to show that we have recognised even the smallest of everyday actions and effort. Let's think about some of the children in your class who rarely, or perhaps never, earn stars or other rewards.

Once a reward has been given, it should never be taken away; it has been earned and that doesn't change even if the child's behaviour does.

It's worth remembering that every child needs to be included in the school's Star of the Week or Celebration Assembly sooner or later, because every child has qualities and behaviours to celebrate. It's important that this is not just seen as working through a list and that it is genuine and is seen as such.

Praise stars

You could think about the positive behaviour children have shown you – for something unconditional, or for simply being themselves – using the praise stars on this page.

For not giving
up when the
maths was
really hard!

collaborative rewards

A collaborative reward system can involve everyone in the class, even the whole school if you choose. It's an excellent way of encouraging co-operation and a sense of community. Many schools in the Nurturing Schools Network have found that collaborative reward systems help the children to be more supportive and encouraging towards each other. Every child can contribute to a shared, earned reward and so everyone's effort, no matter how small, is appreciated by the whole group.

Collaborative reward systems make it easy to recognise other activities that contribute to a positive environment, such as people helping others, being polite, being friendly, trying hard and overcoming setbacks.

Here are some 'top tips' to consider for your collaborative rewards:

- Use a theme to enable concentrating on one behaviour at a time, such as a Listening Week or Tidy Week
- Link the reward system to a particular subject and design a chart with that in mind
- Think of ideas that will allow each member of the school community to earn a reward - One school caretaker leaves a smiley face on the whiteboard of every classroom that has been left clean and tidy and the children look out for it each day to see if they have earned it
- Always have a pot of gems/dinosaurs/pom poms on the go throughout the day; you can add to it in every lesson or activity which is a great way to remind you to be more positive too! It also keeps up momentum

- Make a reward chart that is visually eye catching (such as petals on a sunflower and they grow their own sunflowers from seeds once complete, or leaves on a kindness tree to earn a picnic)
- Make sure that every child takes part in the reward regardless of how many petals, leaves or gems they have contributed

The Classroom Handbooks give lots more ideas and children always enjoy coming up with their own, too. It just needs to be fun; it doesn't needs to take a lot of time or expense. Here are some examples from the Classroom Handbooks:

Smartphone (to reward good listening)

Reward good listening skills with an enlarged outline of a smartphone on a classroom display board. Children are invited to colour in one section at a time when they are noticed using excellent listening skills. Once the entire outline has been filled in, the children may take turns to suggest music to play in class as an opportunity to encourage music appreciation and understanding.

Roman mosaic (to reward co-operative teamwork)

To connect with classroom work on the Romans you could create a Roman mosaic reward chart. A piece of squared paper is stuck onto each table in the classroom to represent tiles on a mosaic. Any child seen co-operating with others is invited to colour in one of the squares on their table; the first table group to have coloured in all its squares earns a reward for the whole class. As they are gradually completed, other tables' mosaics may be added to create a wall display.

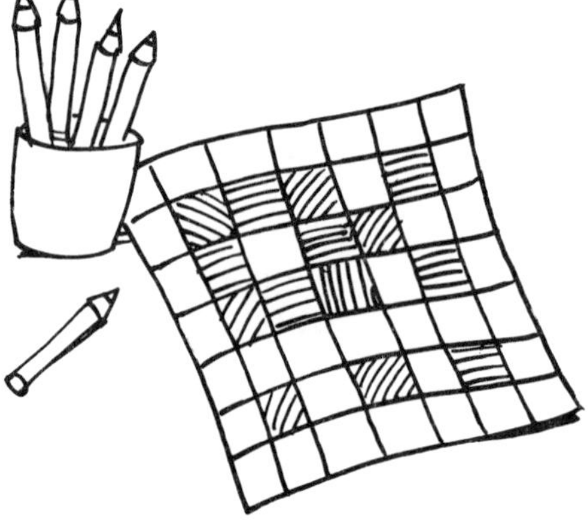

Checklist

- [ ] Remind yourself of the steps for giving praise effectively
- [ ] If you're feeling strong, try inviting a colleague who works alongside you to keep a tally chart of your negative and positive comments over the course of a session –or even a day.
- [ ] Make a list of five ways that a child in your class could earn praise for doing, focusing on the effort involved.
- [ ] Plan to build praise messages into the class routine as a weekly activity throughout the year, so that every child – and adult – experiences it.
- [ ] Design a collaborative reward system with your class.
- [ ] One of the challenges of positive behaviour management is to make sure that children get more attention for their good behaviour than they do for any unhelpful behaviour. The ideas in this chapter will help with this mammoth task!
- [ ] There is also a place for penalties, of course, to be used in response to poor behaviour. We will look more closely at a range of these later in the book.

The Staffroom

"I've never thought about involving the whole school in a reward system. I need to think about using rewards for staff too. We could earn pieces of cake on a chart and then take turns to bake one for the staffroom when the chart is complete!"

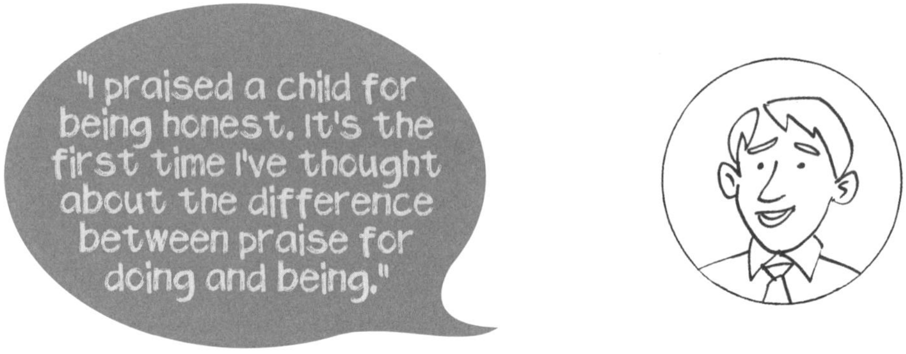

"I praised a child for being honest. It's the first time I've thought about the difference between praise for doing and being."

"I've been using my marble jar for years now so it might be quite fun to think of a new reward system."

"I think I'll buy some praise postcards, so I can post them to parents every now and then."

Extra notes on Chapter 4

Chapter 5: Personal Power, Self-esteem and Choices and Consequences

Introducing Personal Power, Self-esteem and Choices and Consequences

Learning how to be self-confident, make good decisions and feel strong inside

All three of the topics explored in this chapter are closely linked, and together they can have a tremendous influence on the way we behave in later life. If we think of them as three points of a triangle we can see how they are connected. We call this the feelings and behaviour triangle.

As you know, the way we think and feel about ourselves – our self-esteem – affects how we feel about the power we have to make choices, and will influence which choices we make. Let's take a closer look at each of these three areas in turn.

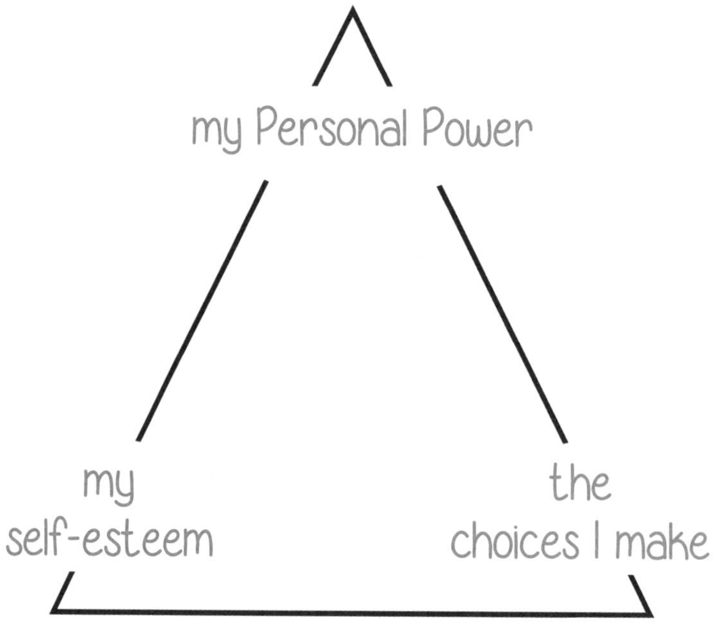

My Personal Power

Personal Power is the emotional strength that we can use to get our needs met and to make choices in our lives

Personal Power is about choosing how we respond to any given situation. If you haven't thought about this idea before it can be hard to grasp, but the first thing to appreciate is that it isn't about being physically strong. Instead, it is the inner, mental strength that we can draw on to face any number of situations in which we find ourselves. If we are going to feel on top of things in our busy lives – at work and at home – we all need to feel that we have some Personal Power.

This section is all about encouraging children at primary school to develop their Personal Power and to feel confident and strong inside. As babies, children need other people to do everything for them and don't yet understand how to make decisions. As children grow older and go to school, they gradually need to have more power and more choice to prepare them for later life. This helps them learn to use their power well – for themselves rather than against others. It's up to us as adults to teach them how.

"At first I was worried about this phrase 'Personal Power'... but now I realise, I have a class of thirty children. I can't afford to let them have too much power or things will get out of control."

It is sometimes true that children can have too much choice and they might use their Personal Power negatively. We talk more about this on page 103. What's important in school is to offer the children a healthy degree of choice, balancing respect for other people with the child's needs.

Encouraging children to use their Personal Power at school is about helping them to become respectful and thoughtful towards their classmates and themselves. It isn't the same as letting them do whatever they want; it's more about them feeling that they have ownership over the actions and the outcomes. A greater sense of internal or Personal Power can reduce the need for using force over others, particularly in the playground.

It may be interesting to relate this to your own life, too. If you are stuck in a traffic jam on the motorway because of roadworks and the traffic is at an absolute standstill, you have no choice but to sit and wait.

If you were in the car, would you lose your temper and allow yourself to rage against the roadworks?

Would you let it put you in a bad mood and ruin your day?

You might well feel powerless, frustrated and anxious about the repercussions of being late for work. It can help to remember that we have the Personal Power to choose how to react to a situation and how to manage the feelings it provokes. We can choose to rage or we can choose to react calmly. Learning how to cope when we are in a stressful situation is an essential life skill. So, we can choose to react positively to the traffic jam by listening to music and staying calm.

Let's have a look at a second scenario, this time with Lauren. Have a look back at the same scenario on page 65. This time she has found a calmer way of entering the classroom and starting the day well.

Children are using their Personal Power all the time in school, and it is always connected to how they are feeling. We can see that Lauren is feeling cross because she has been dropped off at school late and has missed playing with her friends before the bell. She might use her Personal Power by refusing to settle down and do her work, or she might choose to arrange to meet her friends at breaktime instead, then settle down quietly to her work.

Of course it isn't only children in school who have a choice about how to use their Personal Power.

Power and powerlessness

We all have a sense of being powerless sometimes. Below are some words that describe how we feel in relation to our own autonomy. Draw a ring around the words that feel familiar to you.

Strong Confident Calm Competent

Helpful Secure Patient

Energetic Relaxed In control

Decisive Clear Healthy

Defeated Scared

Overwhelmed Tearful Anxious

Aggressive Insecure Violent Silent Paralysed

Angry Useless Desperate

If you are comfortable with the power you have and your ability to have a say in what happens to you, you'll probably have ringed a number of the words in the top box. If you have ringed several of the words in the bottom box, perhaps you feel that too many decisions are being made for you and that you have no control over what is happening to you. These words show us the more negative effects of feeling powerless.

This feeling of powerlessness can be particularly strong in a school where children have to conform to a highly organised day. Think about the children in your class and how these words might apply to them. If a number of the words from the bottom box remind you of a particular child, it is likely that they feel powerless and lack self-esteem.

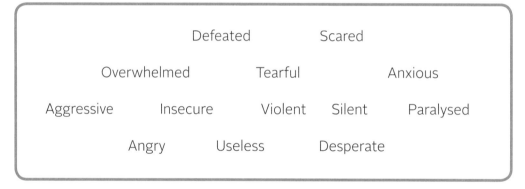

Too much power

The flip side of the coin is that a child can also be given too much power. This might allow them more independence and responsibility than they can handle. It could make them over-serious and worried about doing the right thing. Being offered too many choices could lead to anxiety and indecision. In a situation where an adult is unwell or absent, a child might try to step in and shoulder all the responsibilities and decision-making onto the adult. Childhood should be about being free of adult responsibilities and gradually taking on more autonomy for the decisions they make.

Think again about the feelings associated with power and powerlessness. If the children you are working with seem comfortable with the amount of power they have, then you are on the right track.

Developing Personal Power

We have explored the benefits of children feeling that they have an appropriate level of power. One way to help is to offer opportunities to develop Personal Power. It's a good use of our own Personal Power to help children learn how to use theirs well.

The consistent use of this phrase 'Personal Power', or phrases like 'inner strength', by all adults in school will help to reinforce the idea that Personal Power helps children to make choices, depending on how they feel about themselves. The aim is to make good choices, as these usually have equally good consequences, which boost self-esteem. Children with low self-esteem can find it hard to use their Personal Power positively, but if you refer to it in the classroom, in assemblies, clubs and the playground, children will see that it is integral to how they behave in school and will get the hang of it.

There is an excellent example of how children can use the vocabulary of Personal Power to describe their choices on page 166.

Let's think a bit more about the areas where we have power and how we can choose to use it in a positive or a negative way. We've left a blank row for you to fill in:

Positive use of Personal Power	**The areas we have power in**	**Negative use of Personal Power**
Mostly healthy, with some treats!	**What we eat**	*All junk food or obsessive dieting*
Go to bed early during the week	**When we sleep**	*Constantly stay up late watching TV*
We make sure we have regular times to do something we enjoy	**Time for ourselves**	*We don't make any time at all, working long hours*
	 **Extra ideas:**	

We can also ask the children to think about the power they have to respond when someone says something unkind. They can use their Personal Power negatively and say something unkind back, or they can use it positively and choose to walk away or not react.

See Chapter 8, (page 168) for an example of how you can explore Personal Power through Circle Time.

My self-esteem

Our self-esteem is shaped in childhood by experiences at home, but teachers have a wonderful opportunity to open a child's eyes to different possibilities and to change patterns of behaviour

Self-esteem is the second element of the Feelings and Behaviour Triangle (page 98). It's how we think and feel about ourselves and is linked to motivation, wellbeing, social responsibility and emotional management. It is a very useful concept for working with children. Thinking about the self-esteem of a particular child can provide great insight into their behaviour and progress at school. Poor behaviour in the classroom can be both a cause and an effect of low self-esteem. Either way, it needs our thoughtful attention.

When working with children whose behaviour is regularly less than acceptable, it is a challenge to improve the behaviour without impacting negatively on their self-esteem. We need to be sure that the strategies we use improve their sense of autonomy and Personal Power while leaving it very clear that their behaviour must improve. The positive discipline strategies outlined in this book are designed to work in this way.

Psychologist Murray White's has conducted work looking at Circle Time as a vehicle to improve self-esteem.

"A healthy level of self-esteem enhances your performance, increases your likelihood of success, is the rocket fuel of motivation and the bedrock of wellbeing and contentment."[9]

9. Magic Circles: Self-Esteem for Everyone in Circle Time, Murray White, 2008

Understanding self-esteem

The five competencies[11] of self-esteem, as listed below, may provide a useful framework. We can use these as a diagnostic tool for understanding why a child might be struggling in a particular area. We've also included some of our ideas and suggestions for how to support children in your care.

A sense of belonging

"Do I belong here?"

Take a class photo and update it when new children join the class. Use maps of the local area to show connections between classmates.

A sense of identity

"Who am I?"

Ask everyone to bring a favourite toy to school to share or tell the class about their favourite sport or hobby.

A sense of security

"Am I safe?"

Use maps of the school site and surrounding area to allow children to mark places where they feel safe and unsafe. Encourage children to talk to an adult if they feel anxious about anything.

A sense of competence

"What can I do?"

Use praise and rewards to boost the children's sense of competence. Recognise and reward achievements outside school.

A sense of purpose

"Where do I want to go?"

Encourage children to dream about their futures. Invite positive role models to school.

11. *For further reading: Reasoner, R (1992) Building Self – Esteem in Elementary Schools and Building Self-esteem in Secondary schools. Consulting Psychologists Press, Palo Alto, CA*

Maybe we need to think about what we can do to boost our own self-esteem and that of the children and young people in our care. It's a really good use of Personal Power to be kind to ourselves.

Our self-esteem can be shaped by messages we have received from others throughout our lives. We know that this influences our use of Personal Power and the choices we make. For example, if we feel that others consider us to be challenging or difficult, this may influence us to behave that way.

One way of thinking about it is to see it as a cycle of behaviour:

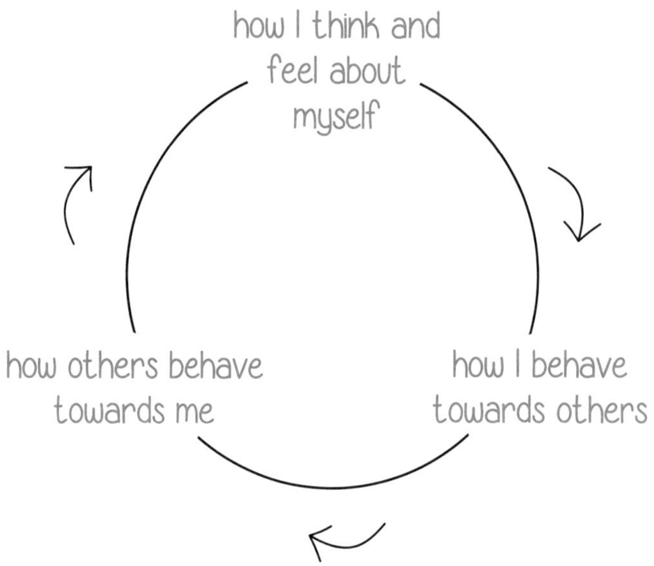

We need to find ways to make this a positive cycle, with healthy self-esteem leading to behaviour that encourages others to behave positively towards us, which will boost our self-esteem.

The weather chart on the next page shows us how attitudes and ways of behaving influence a child's attitudes, behaviour and self-esteem. If a child has experienced lots of input from the stormy side of the weather chart, they may show some of the negative behaviour at the bottom of the chart. So if we can give them lots of experiences on the sunny side, we may help the child feel better about themselves.

How To Increase Self-Esteem

Boundaries * Listening * Praise * Fairness * Consistency

Criticism
Shouting
Mimicking
Arrogance
Put downs
Teasing
Verbal abuse
Smacking
Tying up
Locking in
No fun
No playing
Neglect
Labelling
Coldness
Rejection
Inconsistency
Distrust
No responsibility
Ignoring child
Not listening
No humour
Favouritism
No choices
No cuddles
Threats
Lack of approval
No praise
Nagging

input from others affects how we feel about ourselves and how we behave

Responsibility
Having fun
Love
Consistency
Respect
Understanding
Being listened to
Being treated as an individual
Kindness
Praise
Playing
Clear rules/ boundaries
Encouragement
Trust
Explanations
Negotiations
Fairness
Acceptance
Empathy
Shared humour
Having a good example
Choices
Rewards & penalties

Guilty
Headaches
Isolated
Tired
Angry
Bullied
Bullies
Stammers
Whinges
Refuses to talk
Won't try
Gives up easily
Depressed
Cries a lot
Lonely
Clingy
Over-keen to please
Blames others
Nail biting
Rebellious
Aggressive
Can't concentrate
Tummy aches
Shy
Disruptive
Feels helpless
Stressed
Introverted
Cheeky
Shouts
Breaks rules
Hits and Fights

resulting behaviour and attitudes in children

Confident: prepared to try
Co-operates
Smiles
Listens
Respectful
Copes with setbacks realistically
Happy
Energetic
Praises others
Makes friends
Enthusiastic
Kind
Usually healthy
Affectionate
Resolves problems peaceably
Can self-praise
Assertive
Relaxed
Empathic
Accepts new challenges
Takes responsibility for actions
Tries hard
Resilient
Glad to please

All behaviour has a reason - it's trying to meet a need

You might want to think about some of the children you are working with and see if you can identify attitudes and behaviour on the chart. While we can all have days with both sunshine and showers in them, if we get stuck on the stormy side then it's likely that we're not receiving as much sunshine as we need.

Thinking about this subject can bring up strong feelings. If your class already enjoys a mostly positive emotional climate, your own happy experiences in childhood will be part of the mix. Or you may feel angry or sad if children disclose experiences which remind you of unhappy times in your own life, or embarrassed if you see your class behaving badly.

Give yourself credit for using the Nurturing Programme to begin to change the emotional climate in your class, as everything you do will help the class see other ways of behaving, which will have a positive impact on the rest of the school. Their growing social skills will be transferred from Circle Time to classroom, from classroom to the dinner hall, from the dinner hall to the playground, and it will be your courage to change which started this happening.

Now have a look at the classroom window.

Classroom window

Why is Jake being so disruptive?

Is it his intention to annoy, or does he feel insecure, or some other feeling that is driving his behaviour?

What can you do to help?

The backstory

Jake dislikes detailed drawing as he tends to make mistakes and people have told him that he isn't very good at drawing. He feels cross, anxious and left out. He thinks that by disrupting the others, he will get them to join him on the mat and play something different.

What you could do to help

It is important to make it clear to Jake that disrupting others by throwing paper is a poor use of Personal Power. It's also more likely to annoy other children than encourage them to play with him. Then suggest that the children work together on the comic.

Ask Jake about the other jobs that creating a comic might involve. You might suggest that the comic needs a title, and you know that Jake will have some great ideas as he is so imaginative. He could write his ideas down on a separate piece of paper while the others are drawing.

Praise all the children for working together and being creative.

We can guide Jake away from the disruptive behaviour, find a way for him to join in and boost his self-esteem by offering praise and recognition and encouraging kind peer interaction.

Ideas for building self-esteem

Use Praise postcards praising children for positive behaviours, as shown in Chapter 4.

You could have 'secret buddies' where children pick 3 or 4 children's names – their 'buddies' – from a hat and write (or give verbally to an adult if they are younger) a positive comment about their buddies which then get shared with the child as a star or balloon for the child to take home.

He helps me to organise my things.
He thinks of brilliant games to play.
He always includes me in football.
He's kind when people hurt themselves.
He smiled at me when I was sad.
He loves animals like me!
He works very hard.
He never shouts.

Workbreaks that build self-esteem

You may remember we introduced the idea of workbreaks in Chapter 2. You may well use them already. Workbreaks are quick activities that will change the energy of a class if they are getting tired and distracted, or are restless and over-excited.

You can introduce work breaks into the day when you need something to change the pace, shift the emotional temperature, break up cliques or fill in time while you wait for latecomers (who are unlikely to be late next time if they find they've missed out on the fun of a workbreak!) They are also an essential element of Circle Time. The Classroom Handbooks are full of workbreaks for every age, to complement every topic in the Nurturing Programme.

Here are some examples that would fit the ideas we have been exploring in this chapter:

Alliteration Affirmation

The group stands in a circle and everyone takes turns to say his/her name, preceding it with a positive adjective about him/herself (e.g. Cool Charlie, Intelligent Ibrahim, Amazing Amelia, etc.)

Eleven

This fits in with the theme of Personal Power and encourages children to feel that they really do have a choice in how they use their Personal Power.

The class stands in a circle and a volunteer counts out loud, starting with '1' and counting no further than '3'. The next person follows on, starting with the next number and counting up – again between one and three numbers. When '11' is reached, the person who says it is 'out' and sits down. The next person begins again with '1'. The last to remain standing is the winner.

Give yourself a Hug

Suggest the children could give themselves a hug by wrapping their arms around their shoulders and gently squeezing.

March to my Beat

The children march around the classroom in time to the beat maintained by a volunteer, using a tambourine or drum. The pace of marching needs to reflect variations in the beat.

The Key to my Heart

The children sit in a circle and pass a key around to music; when the music stops, the child with the key says, "The key to my heart is..." and names one of his/her favourite things (e.g. swimming, chocolate ice cream, Harry Potter books, etc.) Repeat as often as time allows.

Carwash

This recognises that everyone deserves to feel good about themselves and so gives a boost to self-esteem.

The class stands in two rows, each facing the other like the brushes in a carwash. They take turns to be the 'car', walking down between the lines and receiving pats on the back, applause, compliments and cheers.

There are more ideas for workbreaks in the Classroom Handbooks and throughout this book and at the back from page 213.

Choices and consequences

Giving children the ability to make choices at school is an essential part of their development

Giving children the ability to make choices is also the third point on our feelings and behaviour triangle. It's very important for children to learn to make thoughtful and effective choices and to find out what happens as a consequence of their decisions. If they aren't given the chance to learn this, they may grow up knowing only how to do as they're told. Alternatively, they may fail to take responsibility for what happens as a result of their decisions.

The ability to make good choices and experience their good outcomes raises self-esteem and helps children become responsible citizens. A lack of choice leads to a feeling of powerlessness which can result in resentment and anti-social behaviour As adults we all want to be in charge of our own lives and steer our own bus rather than be a helpless passenger hiding on the back seat!.

Parent Governor
"I think some children have too much choice and as a result they can be very demanding."

As we have discussed, children are empowered by choice but it must be managed by adults so that it is appropriate and limited. Demanding behaviour comes from too little or too much choice.

Choices need to have clear boundaries and you might like to refer back to the section on boundaries in Chapter 2, page 40.

No choice

I tell Jake that he has a choice either he does what I say right now or he misses football.

It would be hard for Jake to recognise this as a choice rather than a threat. In this chapter we will explore another way of explaining this that will help Jake understand how to make responsible choices.

Choices and consequences

Jake, you have a choice. You can either put your kit in the laundry basket, or you can leave it on the floor...
...If you put it in the basket, I'll wash it and you can go to football. If you leave it on the floor, I won't wash it and you'll miss football...
...It's up to you - it's your choice.

Understanding how our behaviour can upset or hurt someone else teaches us that we need to regulate our behaviour and consider other people. It's a vital social skill that will be tested time and time again when we are adults. If we make a poor choice we learn that we have to live with the consequences.

Choices and consequences as a strategy supporting behaviour for learning

Children need to be helped to understand that they have a choice about how they behave. Hopefully you are beginning to see how Personal Power, self-esteem and choices and consequences are linked together. Learning to think about behaviour choices helps children learn self-discipline and gain an important life skill. Used well, choices and consequences will keep you in charge while giving a child appropriate power. For instance, a carefully phrased choice and consequence can dramatically reduce arguments and confrontations.

Have a look at the following cartoon. **Why do you think Lauren is reacting the way she does to Mrs Johnson? How do you think Lauren is feeling now?**

Come along Lauren – do as I say right now... get on with your work and stop distracting Maya!
No! I won't!

Now let's have look at the strategy of choices and consequences to see how this will help manage Lauren's behaviour positively. It's very easy to get locked into conflict with children. You've probably all experienced a situation where you have asked a child to do something and they have refused point blank to do it. We suggest that the way to avoid this is to follow a simple set of responses, as laid out on the next page. It's an excellent way of defusing conflict.

By offering choices and consequences we can remind children of their Personal Power, and help them understand the consequences of their decisions.

Giving choices and consequences

Lauren, you have a choice.

You can either work quietly...
(helpful behaviour choice)

...or you can carry on chatting
(unhelpful behaviour choice)

If you choose to work quietly...
(helpful behaviour choice)

...then you can stay at this table with your friends.
(helpful consequence)

...If you choose to carry on chatting...
(unhelpful behaviour choice)

...then you'll need to sit on your own so you don't distract anyone.
(unhelpful consequence)

It's up to you - it's your choice." *(Remember this bit; it's crucial to say)*

"Ok... I'll stop chatting so I can stay here."

By stating that the child has a choice both at the beginning and end of this strategy is a useful way of reminding children that they are using Personal Power. Sometimes, the use of two options for the positive behaviour choice can work as an effective distraction:

"Would you like to sit here... or there?"

Steps for choices and consequences

1. Be clear about the helpful and unhelpful choices that a child can make about their behaviour and try not to refer to the choices as good, bad, right or wrong as that introduces a judgemental tone
2. Be clear about the helpful and unhelpful consequences that will follow
3. Relate consequences directly to behaviour
4. Choose consequences that mean something to the child
5. Avoid giving a choice where there isn't one
6. Avoid threats or ultimatums
7. Try to have a bank of consequences thought through in advance that can be adapted to the situation - and that are easy to follow through with
8. Avoid asking for an instant answer: give the child 'take up' time and, if appropriate, encourage the child to reflect on the choice they made at a later stage

Did you know... ?

Descriptions of choices as good, bad, right or wrong introduce a judgmental tone. To keep the empowering element of this strategy, try referring to them as helpful or unhelpful choices.

Try using the language of 'helpful' and 'unhelpful' choices as shown below.

.... you have a choice.
(child's namc)

You can either ....
(helpful behaviour choice)

...or you can ....
(unhelpful behaviour choice)

If you choose ....
(helpful behaviour choice)

...then ....
(helpful consequence)

If you choose ....
(unhelpful behaviour choice)

...then ....
(unhelpful consequence)

It's up to you - it's your choice.
(It's crucial to finish by saying this)

Choices and consequences

Here are a few more examples:

Finishing a maths activity

You have a choice. You can either finish your maths now or you can carry on sharpening your pencil. If you choose to finish your maths now then you'll have the whole of breaktime free. If you choose to carry on sharpening your pencil then you'll need to spend 10 minutes of breaktime finishing your maths.

It's up to you – it's your choice.

Listening during carpet time

You have a choice. You can either put your hand up when you have something to say or you can call out. If you choose to put your hand up then I'll know I need to listen to you. If you choose to call out then I may not be able to hear what you have to say.

It's up to you – it's your choice.

Behaving in the playground

You have a choice. You can either be a good sport or you can lose your temper. If you choose to be a good sport, you can carry on playing football for the rest of breaktime. If you choose to lose your temper, then you'll need to stop playing football and do something else instead.

It's up to you – it's your choice.

The strategies we have already explored in earlier chapters will be very helpful in supporting children to develop a sense of self-esteem, their personal power and the choices they make. *Here are some reminders for all three:*

Checklist

- [ ] Treat children with respect.
- [ ] Give them chances to succeed.
- [ ] Praise them for positive behaviours and the effort they apply to their work.
- [ ] Listen and talk to them.
- [ ] Honour their feelings.
- [ ] Allow them to learn from their mistakes.
- [ ] Encourage them to take responsibility for their decisions.
- [ ] Make clear to a child the positive and negative uses of personal power and how this relates to them.
- [ ] Consequences should always be clear, fair and appropriate. Consider having a 'bank' of consequences to hand that are easy to implement.

The Staffroom

"I can see how choices and consequences can have a really positive impact on behaviour in the school, and give the staff another helpful strategy to use."

"I think I might try it out on my husband!"

"I use choices and consequences all the time for the whole class and it works well. They feel they have a positive input into what goes on."

"I'm glad I tried choices and consequences with Lauren, instead of getting into stalemate with her repeated "No". Using a choice and consequence helps me stay calm."

Extra notes on Chapter 5

Chapter 6: Managing and Dealing with Difficult Feelings

Difficult Feelings

Difficult feelings are okay; it's what we do with them that matters

In Chapter 3 we talked about feelings and how important it is to help children to tune in to them. As we know, emotional literacy is about being able to identify, accept and healthily express a full range of feelings. No feelings are bad, although we can sometimes be made to feel that they are. Ignoring or disapproving of a difficult feeling doesn't make it go away. In fact, it just adds other complex feelings such as guilt or shame to the mix.

Acknowledging and expressing difficult feelings is the first step in dealing with them; we can then move on to thinking about the situation that provoked them and what, if anything, we need to do either about the situation itself or about our response to it.

Anger can be one of the most powerful and difficult emotions to handle. It rises to the surface for many reasons, often when we feel threatened. Unfortunately, as children, many adults were made to feel bad if they showed any anger. As a result they may find it hard to tolerate anger in other adults or in children. Others may have witnessed anger being acted out through violence towards themselves or to others, so may also be afraid of it or perhaps imitate it in their own life.

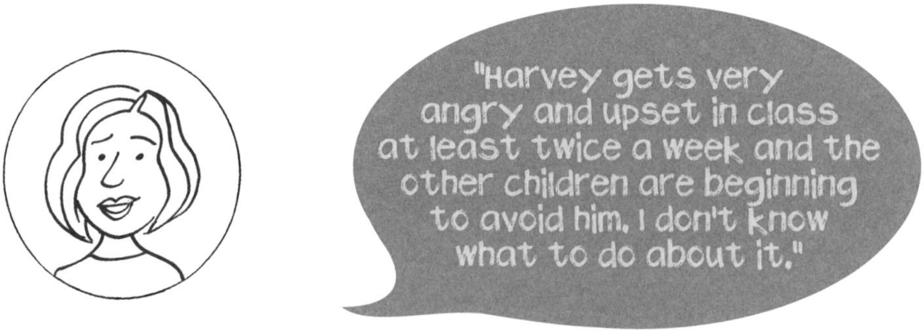

"Harvey gets very angry and upset in class at least twice a week and the other children are beginning to avoid him. I don't know what to do about it."

Anger is a secondary emotion. It's a reaction to fear, threat or hurt of some kind; a protective reaction or survival instinct. Trying to identify the problem and the emotions that lie behind the anger can sometimes be more helpful than focusing entirely on the anger itself, though it is usually possible to do this only when the storm of anger has passed.

Did you know...

about the speed of adrenaline?

In the first 10 seconds after we react to a threat, the primitive emotional centre of the brain, the amygdala, releases a surge of adrenaline to help us fight, flee (flight) or freeze. This is our irrational response. At this pointwe become very alert and blood rushes to our arms and hands to prepare us to lash out, and to our legs to help us run away. A fearful, frightened or humiliated child is likely to run away, hide or act out to avoid the source of his/her fear. After 10 seconds the rational part of the brain starts to function, looking for ways to discharge the adrenaline. It can take up to 8 hours for adrenaline to disperse and it will accumulate if we are repeatedly in stressful situations.[12]

Those who have not learned to control their aggressive reactions by the time they start school enter a vicious circle of negative interactions where rejection from their peers, because of their aggressive behaviour, leads to more aggression.

Such children need lots of help to learn alternatives to physical aggression at a time when it is developmentally appropriate, i.e., during pre-school years.

When we're trying to manage difficult behaviour in the classroom, it's easy to forget about or overlook the strong feelings that triggered it. It may be helpful to focus on why a child shows anger and how other feelings can contribute to aggressive behaviour. An understanding or empathic response to a child who is troubled or frustrated can really help to dispel the negative feelings.

12. For further reading on how the amygdala functions and it's role in child development see Gerdhart, S Why Love Matters: How affection shapes a baby's brain, Routledge 2015

Questions to ask yourself:

- When you are angry how do you respond?
- When you are angry what else do you feel?
- When you were a child, how did you feel if someone close to you was angry?
- Are there certain situations that trigger anger in your class?
- Are there certain children who display anger on a regular basis?

Anger may build up gradually or it may flare up unexpectedly over something that may seem quite insignificant. Anger can manifest itself in different ways: for example a child 'playing up', refusing to connect with you, being verbally abusive (both loud and quiet) and through physical aggression. If a child displays anger in the classroom it is very likely to have been provoked by other feelings such as anxiety, fear or frustration which have combined to produce an angry reaction.

This chapter will explore triggers for anger and how other feelings such as anxiety, jealousy and frustration can build up to anger. This helps us to respond more empathically to a child who is angry and disruptive in school.

Safe ways to deal with anger in school

We know that it helps children at school to release anger and let it go. If there is any risk of a child hurting themselves or others, we have to take steps to contain – and protect others from – the situation. Your school will have guidelines and procedures for how to manage a child who needs to be physically removed from a situation. If possible, it's helpful to spot when feelings are building up before they reach boiling point.

If there is a child who is displaying anger in school, the following steps offer safe ways to help both them and their classmates cope with their anger, and manage those feelings before they explode.

Helping to manage difficult feelings

- Make time to listen to their side of the story
- Lead the class in a workbreak
- Have a stress ball available (or a soft toy to hug in Early Years Foundation Stage and Key Stage 1 classes at all times
- Offer a glass of water (the swallow reflex is very soothing)
- Suggest they take three slow breaths and count to ten (you can too!)
- Take them away from the cause of their anger to somewhere safe where you can talk without the rest of the class being involved
- Suggest that they scribble an angry picture
- Provide some clay or Play-Doh™ to knead
- Suggest they do some physical exercise
- Remember that behaviour can escalate throughout the day, so track back through the events that led up to a display of anger
- Use Time Out to Calm Down (see page 133)
- Do relaxation or meditation exercises with the whole class (see page 137))

Afterwards, we can take some time to think about what triggers the anger. A Difficult Feelings Backtrack (page 131) can sometimes help everyone understand why their feelings got the better of them; it's also a good way to help young children learn the skill of reflection. *Is it at a particular time of day, is it a particular lesson? Is it because another child has touched a nerve with something they said?* Other members of your team may have insights, too, from the way this child behaves with them.

Physical exercise

It's important to find ways of discharging adrenaline and cortisol, the hormones involved in stress building up to anger. Anger-release exercises will help a child to calm down and can involve the whole class. If we have noticed that breaktimes or other parts of the school day are causing problems that are brought back into the classroom, we could introduce a game or workbreak before the next activity. This could help provide a transition into the classroom environment, allow any difficult feelings to be released and change the energy and mood of your class (see also Chapter 9 on problem solving).

Here are two possible workbreaks that you can use to release anger. You will find others in the Classroom Handbooks. The Popcorn workbreak we suggested in Chapter 2, (page 129) might be useful here, too.

A simple relaxation activity

Stand in a circle and stamp your feet in turn. At the same time, flex your hands by making a tight fist and then stretching out your fingers as far as they will go.

Rub your hands together rapidly until they are warm.

Hold them against your face (over eyes and cheeks) and breathe in deeply.

To let in the light gradually, spread the fingers and bring the hands down slowly over your cheeks.

Thunderstorm

For the thunderstorm, begin each action for the child on your left to copy while you keep going, and so on around the circle until the action returns to you, whereupon you start the next action. Everyone in the circle continues their action until the new one reaches them.

1. Gently rub palms together
2. Tap two fingers on palm of one hand
3. Clap hands
4. Slap hands on thighs
5. Slap hands on thighs and stamp feet
6. Slap hands on thighs
7. Clap hands
8. Tap two fingers on palm of one hand
9. Gently rub palms together
10. Cross your arms to finish

A difficult feelings backtrack

Anger often erupts as the final stage of a chain of events that can start hours, or even days, before the anger is displayed. It can help us understand an angry child if we try and track these events as far back as we can. This technique encourages you to think about the feelings that might lie behind certain behaviour.

Let's track back through a scenario where Jake has been sent to Mrs Wilson's office and immediately kicked over a chair. It may seem as though this is an extreme reaction with no obvious cause, and Jake will need to understand that it is not acceptable. However, after dealing with Jake, Mrs Wilson takes time to track back through what happened to see why Jake's behaviour escalated to that point. We can see what she discovered by tracking back from scenes 6-1 in the pictures below.

The backtrack technique is another great way of using empathy as a strategy for managing difficult behaviour. By understanding the different feelings that Jake experienced – from loneliness and rejection in the first scenario to frustration and anger in the final scene in the headteacher's office –backtracking allows the teacher to intercept feelings along the way before they grow into extreme feelings that trigger disruptive behaviour. The teacher could decide to involve the two girls, so that they can see the role they played in the escalation of his feelings and behaviour. They could also encourage other friendship groups and suggest Jake uses some of the ideas listed on page 129. Jake still needs to know that his behaviour is not acceptable, and the empathic recognition of his feelings may help him to find a way of managing his feelings so that he avoids getting into trouble and keeps him and others safe.

Time out to Calm Down

Time Out to Calm Down is a way of helping children and adults when emotions are running high, by offering a cooling-off period that gives everyone a chance to calm down

Time Out
to calm down

You may be familiar with the technique of Time Out to Calm Down, and there are several different approaches to using this strategy. The Nurturing Programme uses Time Out to Calm Down as an opportunity to manage difficult feelings rather than as a punishment. It should never be imposed aggressively or in a way that is humiliating to the child. Time Out to Calm Down gives the child a cooling-off period away from the source of upset, while also allowing those around them some breathing space.

When we think about it in this way, we don't have to remove the child from the classroom or exclude them from an activity, unless of course the situation is becoming dangerous. If you have enough space in the classroom, you might want to create a chill-out corner or calming-down space with, for example, a bean-bag. A sandtimer is particularly useful for keeping time and soothing the child.

Time out to calm Down works best when a child doesn't want to miss 'Time In'

Time Out to Calm Down is a two-stage process.

With children up to the age of 8-9 years, it's an effective strategy for dealing calmly with difficult behaviour;

With children over 9 years who are more mature it becomes more pre-emptive, i.e. they are encouraged to use Time Out to Calm Down for themselves as a way of calming down before they lose control.

The ideas of Time Out to Calm Down can be introduced as part of the classroom agreement (page 42), when discussing boundaries, rewards and penalties with children.

Steps for Preparing Time Out to Calm Down

1. Explain the idea of Time Out to Calm Down clearly to the class
2. Discuss what behaviour will lead to Time Out to Calm Down
3. Pick a Time Out to Calm Down place that is suitable, e.g., a quiet corner of the classroom
4. Decide how long Time Out to Calm Down will last (30 secs to 2 mins)

Steps for Giving Time out to Calm Down

When an agreement has been broken:

1. Give a clear warning and a reminder about the agreement. Give one more chance, unless physical violence has been involved, in which case Time Out to Calm Down should be given immediately, making it a short term consequence
2. If the rule is broken again, tell the child to go to the Time Out to Calm Down spot
3. Ignore all comments, promises, arguing or pleas
4. Remind the child how long Time Out to Calm Down will last for
5. Remind the child that Time Out to Calm Down will only start when they are sitting quietly
6. Set a timer for the agreed time
7. When Time Out to Calm Down is over, praise the child for taking it well and invite them to re-join the class

Later - and if age-appropriate:

1. Ask the child how they were feeling just before the behaviour that led to Time Out to Calm Down. Use the backtrack technique on page 131 to help you understand why they were angry. Explain why their behaviour is unacceptable
2. Ask the child to suggest what they could do differently if the same situation came up again
3. Follow through with any appropriate negative consequence

Time out... to have a think

The diagrams below are another way of helping an older child (8+) reflect on past behaviour and feelings and how they might act and feel differently in the future.

This is most effective when used at least a day after the incident.

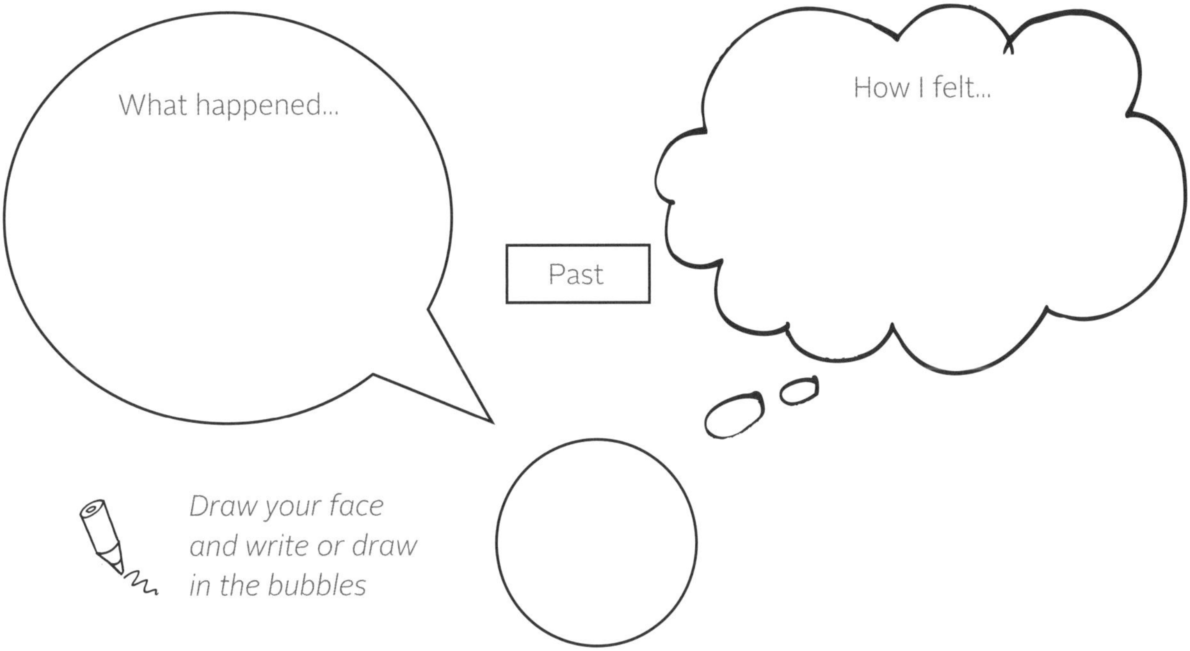

Time Out to Calm Down is a very flexible strategy for use around school, in the playground, in breakfast club and so on. It helps when schools have a consistent policy for using Time Out to Calm Down so that all the children understand what is going to happen and that it is to help them manage their feelings. As we have seen, it can be one of the ways we manage our anger and it can also be one of the consequences that we suggest if we are using the choice and consequences strategy discussed in Chapter 5.

Time Out to Calm Down is also great to use for ourselves! If we feel our emotional temperature rising, we can find a minute to breathe slowly, count to ten, look out of the window or drink some water. We can use lunchbreaks to find a few minutes to help us calm down and re-focus before going back into the classroom or playground.

Classroom window

Why is Lauren unable to sit still? Why does she appear to be disruptive so early in the day? What can you do to help?

The backstory

Lauren's parents are separated. Her dad lives a long way from the school and when Lauren goes to stay with him once a week they have to take a car journey through heavy traffic to get to school. She always arrives late and never has time to catch up with her friends before class begins. She has not had any time to release any pent-up energy and anxiety and finds it difficult to sit still on the carpet and concentrate.

What you could do to help

We might find time to ask Lauren about her morning and use the backtrack technique (see page 131) to work out what might be going on. Once you have established that each week she has to travel to school on a long car journey, you could think about ways of allowing her to let off some steam on arrival. Perhaps every Wednesday could start with a workbreak for the whole class, or you might think of a small task that Lauren might do once a week that involves going to the school office. She might choose to spend her first few minutes in the 'chill-out corner'. This would help Lauren to settle in without making her feel more frustrated and constrained, and it would help your day start more easily too.

Relaxation Holiday

The range of Centre for Emotional Health training courses introduce many relaxation exercises that help children and adults let go of difficult feelings. One of the most useful is Relaxation Holiday. This exercise is best done with a class that has already explored difficult feelings through Circle Time. Ask the class to sit or lie comfortably on the floor with enough distance between them so as not to distract each other. Invite them to close their eyes and then slowly read out the following. Sit comfortably, start with a few slow, easy breaths and begin to relax... *and now let your mind create these sensations.*

Imagine the colours of the sky in a beautiful sunset.

Imagine the sound of water flowing in a stream.

Imagine the smell of a bonfire on a crisp autumn day.

Imagine the feel of smooth, clean sheets.

Imagine the smell of a field of grass in the hot summer sun.

Imagine the stars and moon in the dark sky on a clear night.

Imagine the taste of a favourite food.

Imagine the sound of a beautiful song.

Imagine the wind blowing on your face.

Imagine floating on the still, shallow water of a peaceful lake.

Notice the feeling of calm and peace, and take time to enjoy it. Then, when you are ready, open your eyes and come back to us here.

There are lots more ideas for relaxation exercises in the Classroom Handbooks and in *The Parenting Puzzle* book.

See the website for more details at **centreforemotionalhealth.org.uk.**

Checklist

☐ Think of five more safe ways for children to release anger at school.

☐ Next time you have an incident at school that involves challenging behaviour, try the backtrack technique and see if it changes the way you might have managed it.

☐ Try one of the anger-release workbreaks we have suggested or the Relaxation Holiday activity. This is a good activity for older children to use to release stress, e.g. before SATS or other tests.

☐ Try taking a Time Out to Calm Down for yourself: it's a great way to manage stress at school.

The Staffroom

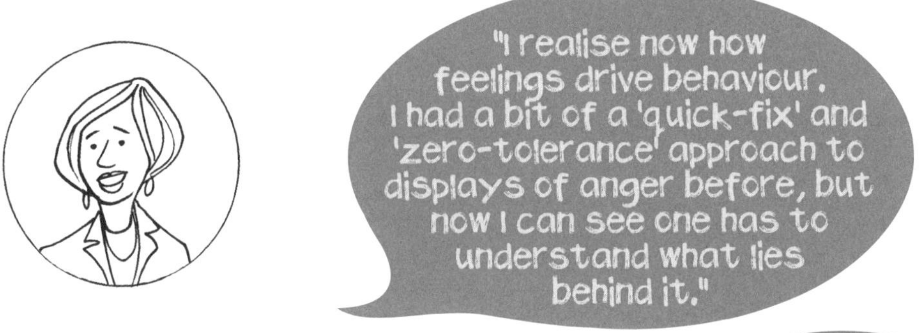

"I realise now how feelings drive behaviour. I had a bit of a 'quick-fix' and 'zero-tolerance' approach to displays of anger before, but now I can see one has to understand what lies behind it."

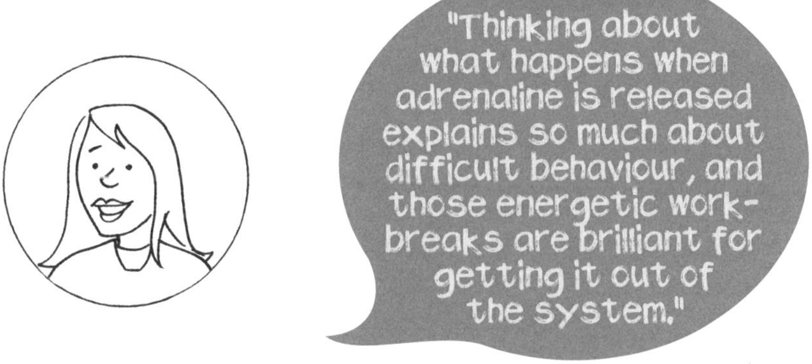

"Thinking about what happens when adrenaline is released explains so much about difficult behaviour, and those energetic work-breaks are brilliant for getting it out of the system."

"Jake finds Time Out to Calm Down so helpful as a place to calm down, and I hear that Lauren in year 6 takes herself to the Time Out to Calm Down zone now without anyone having to ask her."

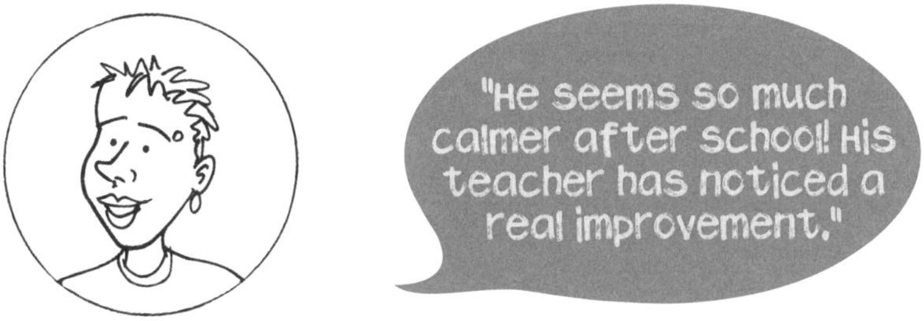

"He seems so much calmer after school! His teacher has noticed a real improvement."

Chapter 7: Ages and Stages and the Effects of Labelling

Ages and stages in children's development

Having appropriate expectations and avoiding labels

Children develop in very different ways and it's best that they do this at their own pace. As we know, some children arrive at primary school already very sociable and ready to make friends; others find it more difficult to be part of a large group.

Some children are already very capable of throwing and catching a ball, while others find it almost impossible because their hand-eye coordination is still developing. All this is perfectly normal development.

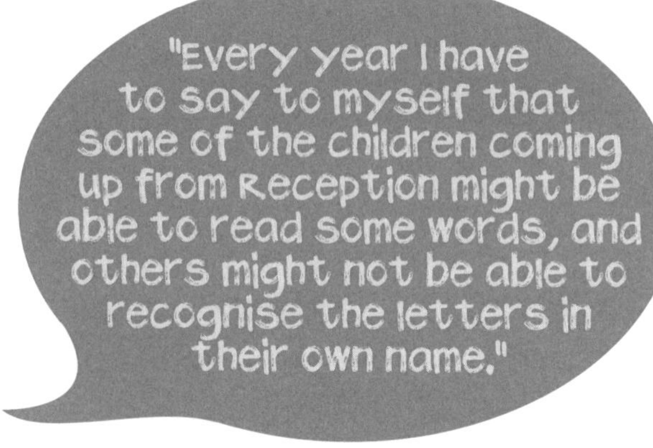

"Every year I have to say to myself that some of the children coming up from Reception might be able to read some words, and others might not be able to recognise the letters in their own name."

It is helpful if our expectations of the children we work with allow for these differences and are tailored to the stage they are at, so that we guide and encourage children to learn and grow. It is unhelpful to make unreasonable demands or to send out messages to a child that suggest they have failed or disappointed others.

A child who is able to do more than we allow them to do might feel frustrated and rebellious; a child who is expected to do more than he or she is ready for might feel inadequate and ashamed. Refer back to Chapter 4 for helpful reminders of how you can do **Guiding without Criticising**.

Managing expectations

To help children to develop in every way – physically, mentally, socially and emotionally – it's best to think of your role as a guiding and supporting one. First we will look at how parents might be controlling or empowering with their children. When it comes to leading the class, we may like to reflect on the difference between controlling and empowering them.

Controlling (unhelpful)

In this scenario, Billy's dad is doing everything for Billy and is over-protective. As a result Billy could become lazy and demanding, or feel helpless and incapable.

Empowering (helpful)

In this scenario, Billy's dad is helping him to acquire practical skills and be responsible. This will help Billy become more capable and learn to use his initiative.

Controlling (unhelpful)

Mr George wants Billy to do well. He thinks he's urging Billy to do better but the message Billy gets is that nothing is ever good enough. Billy could become so discouraged that he stops trying, or may become over-anxious about achievement to the point of being perfectionist.

Empowering (helpful)

In this final example, Billy's teacher has reasonable expectations of Billy and enjoys and encourages his success. Billy takes pride and pleasure in his work and learns to be realistic about his own achievements. He appreciates that self-esteem is not dependent on high marks.

These examples remind us of the power of language to set expectations for and empower the child. It's always useful to stop and consider the words we use – and this is true for how we speak to our colleagues, friends and family too.

The effects of labelling

When we are children we are often given labels by the adults around us. These labels can be used so much that they come to define who we are and we feel we must live up to their name. It's the repetition that turns an observation into a label. Sometimes the labels are quite negative.

Remember: labels inform our self-concept. Difficult labels can be a major factor in lowering self-esteem. Sometimes children have positive labels, and these too can define our self-image and others' expectations of us. A child who is labelled "well-behaved" may suppress some of their feelings in order to conform to this label.

What about me?

Think of the labels that you might have carried as a child and how you felt about them. On a separate piece of paper write down the labels that were put on you and the feelings attached to them. It may be quite painful to remember how restricting or even hurtful these were.

Once you've done this, and reflected on it for a moment, scribble out the label(s) you wrote down: they are other people's opinions, are very out of date and don't represent who you really are.

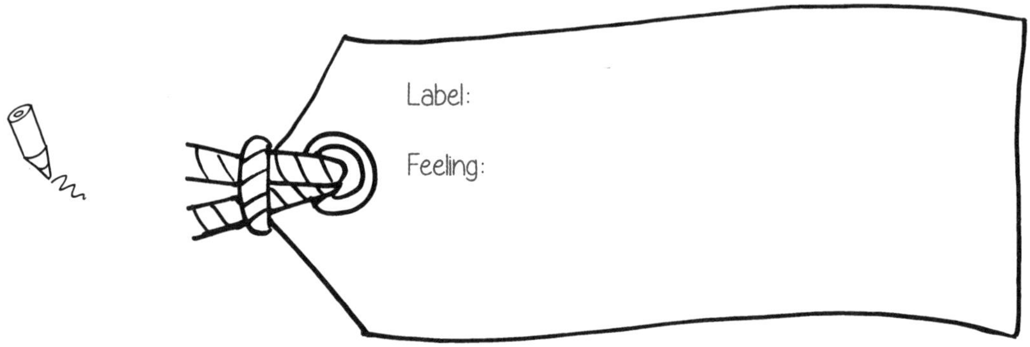

Now, think of any labels that the children you work with might be carrying and make a list. If you feel these are negative labels, cross them out and replace them with something positive.

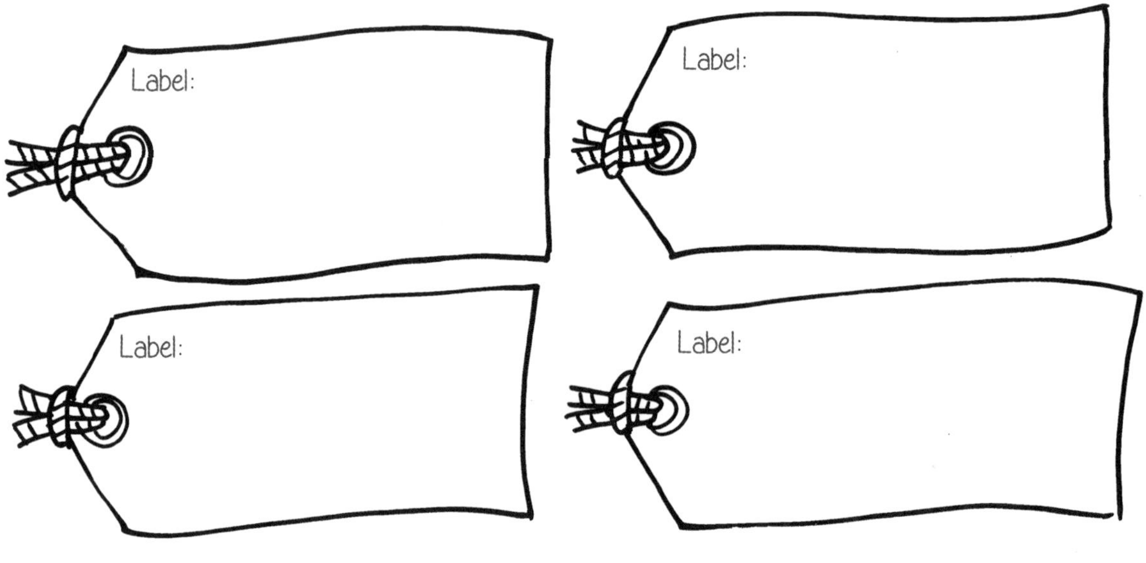

The ways we learn

There are many ways in which teachers think about how children learn: identifying children's needs, fostering their creativity and developing their potential by considering styles of learning.

Theories of learning are constantly evolving, with the latest neuroscience research offering fresh insights into the function, structure and workings of the human brain. Some of the most common and widely used learning theories are therefore contested but are nevertheless useful to consider. These theories include:

Howard Gardner's Multiple Intelligences model

Gardner's model suggests that intelligence is not confined to one general ability but looks instead at nine modalities including spatial, linguistic, musical, interpersonal, intrapersonal, naturalistic, existential and logical-mathematical.

Fleming's VAK approach

Fleming's approach considers Visual, Auditory and Kinaesthetic ways of learning.

Kolb's Experiential Learning Theory

Kolb's theory views experiential learning as a cyclical process of having a concrete experience, with learners accommodating (feeling and doing), diverging (feeling and watching), converging (thinking and doing) and assimilating (thinking and watching).

Despite being contested, these models of learning still have much to offer. From practice, from listening to teachers and children, and from our own learning experiences, we know that a variety of learning activities is crucial, exposing children to new and different ways of learning and maintaining pace and variety in classrooms.

The Circle time activities in our Classroom Handbooks, and the pedagogical methods and strategies included in this book seek to illustrate the various approaches to learning we might include when working with children. From the big-picture learner to the child who finds it helpful to be physically active; and from the detail-focused child to the pupil who needs written instructions, planning for children with different learning preferences not only helps all children engage with learning, but can also help us as teachers be more creative and varied in our teaching.

For further reading see:

To find out more about Fleming's VARK model (R stands for ReadWrite) see the website:

www.vark-learn.com

Frames of Mind, The Theory of Multiple Intelligences

Gardner, H, Basic Books 2011

Experiential Learning: Experience as the Source of Learning and Development

Kolb, D, Prentice Hall 1983

Checklist

- [ ] Consider your expectations of children and adults in your life, and the language you use to express them.
- [ ] Check out your knowledge on age-appropriate developments on the next page.
- [ ] Think about the Nurturing Programme topic you are planning to teach this week and work on an approach to it that will be appropriate for different types of learners.
- [ ] List some ways you can empower children to make their own decisions.

Ages and stages quiz

 Checking out our knowledge of what to expect from a
~~child as they grow from baby to 12-years-old~~

Communicating effectively with parents is an important job for all schools. If
parents misunderstand the work you are doing, or have inappropriate expectations
of what their child is capable of, they can make your role very difficult.

In Chapter 7 we have been looking at ages and stages, and how to understand and
manage expectations built of the children in your school. We've included a quiz
to give a general idea of what to expect as children develop and grow. Of course,
there's no such thing as an average child.

The lists on the next two pages offer a selection of skills and attitudes that
children learn as they grow up, in school and at home. At what age do you think an
average child might be able to do these? Try filling in the ages.

0 - 2 years / 2 - 4 years / 4 - 7 years / 7 - 9 years / 9 - 12 years

0 - 2	begins to use words		giggles about toilet talk
	can prepare/make simple snacks		has a 900-word vocabulary
	chooses own friends		helps care for pets
	concentrates for up to five mins		helps put away toys
	develops opinions and explains views on self and society		gets bag and coat ready independently
	does simple ironing		identifies colours
	explores body parts		is able to use the toilet
	faces new challenges		is able to balance on one foot
	fears strangers		is able to catch a ball
	gets dressed without help		is able to collaborate

- [ ] is able to cross road safely alone
- [ ] is able to draw a person
- [ ] is able to make amends
- [ ] is aware of gender/sex
- [ ] is appreciative of another point of view
- [ ] is careful with hot things
- [ ] lays/clears table
- [ ] makes simple choices
- [ ] is beginning to be give empathic responses
- [ ] makes a cup of tea while supervised
- [ ] makes art/craftwork on own
- [ ] makes bed
- [ ] makes responsible choices
- [ ] manages pocket money
- [ ] manages Time Out to Calm Down for self
- [ ] may adopt special comfort object
- [ ] may be jealous of siblings
- [ ] may have an imaginary friend
- [ ] needs company, warm words and gentle touch
- [ ] needs peace and quiet
- [ ] needs privacy
- [ ] plays sociably
- [ ] prepares own lunchbox
- [ ] puts toys away independently
- [ ] realises how their own behaviour impacts on others
- [ ] recognises the difference between deliberate and accidental hurt
- [ ] responsible for doing homework
- [ ] rides a bike
- [ ] sets personal goals
- [ ] shares toys, belongings and activities
- [ ] sorts out minor squabbles
- [ ] takes responsibility for school tasks, e.g, the class register
- [ ] tells the time
- [ ] understands jokes
- [ ] understands "No"
- [ ] understands that feelings affect behaviour
- [ ] uses child's scissors
- [ ] uses a knife and fork
- [ ] washes hands before lunch

The answers

0-2 years

begins to use words

explores body parts (also 4-7)

fears strangers

may adopt special comfort object (also 4-7, and even 7-9)

may be jealous of siblings (true of all ages)

needs company, warm words and gentle touch (true of all ages)

needs peace and quiet (true of all ages)

understands "No"

2-4 years

concentrates for up to five minutes

has a 900-word vocabulary

helps put away toys

identifies colours

is dry at night (also 4–7)

makes simple choices

may have an imaginary friend

plays sociably (3+)

shares toys and belongings (3+)

uses child's scissors

4-7 years

chooses own friends

gets dressed without help (5-6)

giggles about toilet talk

is able to catch a ball

is able to draw a person

uses a knife and fork

washes hands before lunch (4+)

helps care for pets (also 7-9)

is able to use the toilet (5)

is aware of gender/sex

is beginning to give empathic responses

lays/clears table (5-7)

put toys away independently (5+)

rides a bike

understands jokes

understands that feelings affect behaviour

7-9 years

faces new challenges

is able to collaborate

is able to make amends

is appreciative of another point of view

makes art/craftwork on own

makes bed

makes responsible choices

manages Time Out to Calm Down for self

prepares own lunchbox

realises how their own behaviour impacts on others

recognises the difference between deliberate and accidental hurt

sorts out minor squabbles

tells the time

9-12 years

develops opinions and explains views on self and society

does simple ironing

gets bag and coat ready independently

is able to cross road safely alone (10+)

is careful with hot things (10-11+)

makes cup of tea while supervised

manages pocket money

needs privacy

responsible for doing homework

responsible for pets

sets personal goals

takes responsibility for school tasks, e.g. the register (9+)

The Staffroom

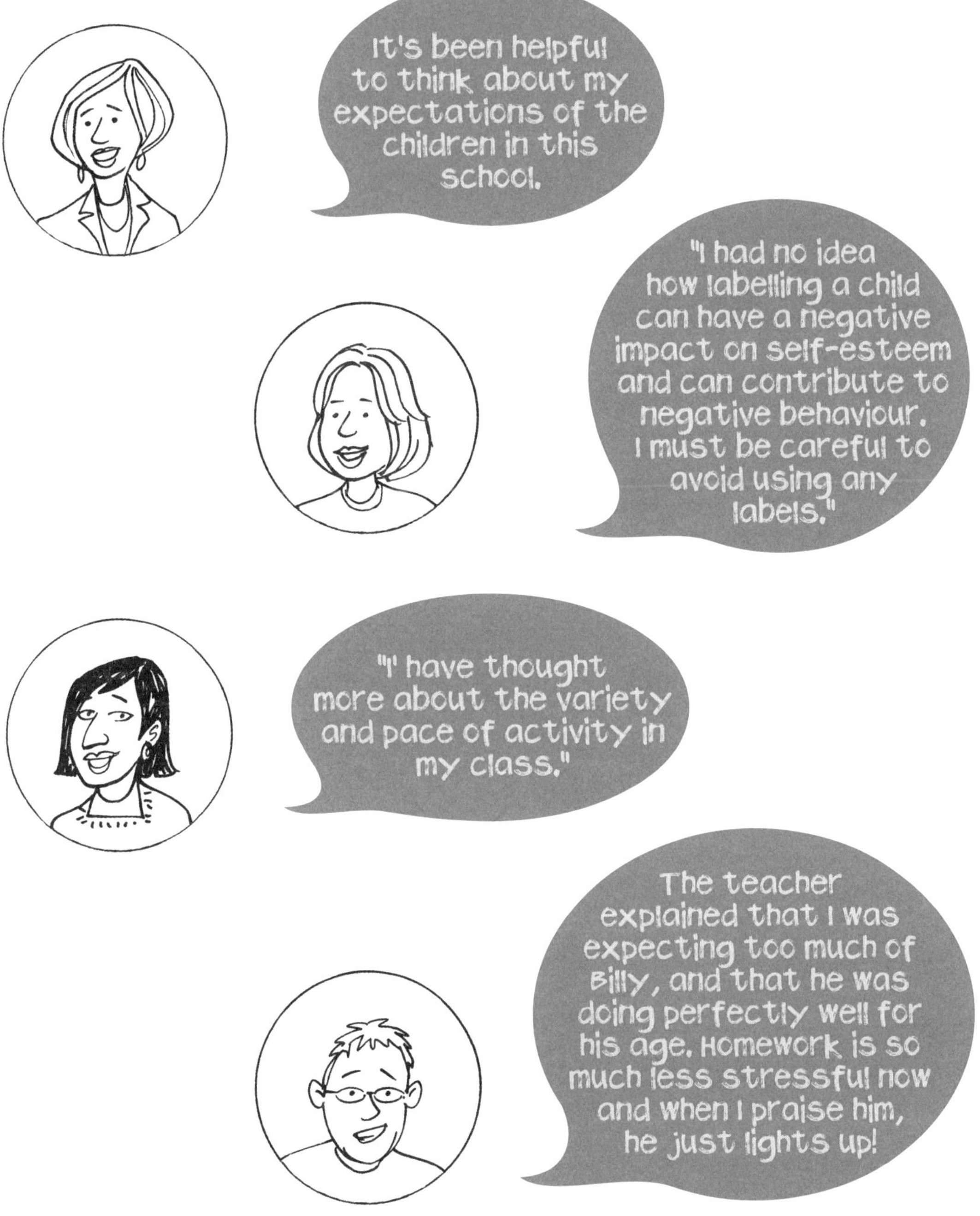

It's been helpful to think about my expectations of the children in this school.
"I had no idea how labelling a child can have a negative impact on self-esteem and can contribute to negative behaviour. I must be careful to avoid using any labels."
"I' have thought more about the variety and pace of activity in my class."
The teacher explained that I was expecting too much of Billy, and that he was doing perfectly well for his age. Homework is so much less stressful now and when I praise him, he just lights up!

Chapter 8: Effective Circle Time

Ideas for effective Circle Time

Learning new ideas for Circle Time and how best to manage it

Used effectively, Circle Time can transform your classroom into a strong, caring and respectful community. It provides children with the necessary basic knowledge, skills and understanding to become emotionally resilient, socially-skilled individuals equipped to make the best of life at school and at home. When we're inviting children to learn about themselves and each other, we are doing far more than just facilitating a discussion: we're opening the door to truly transformative learning.

Circle Time is the part of the school week when children can learn how to understand themselves and their peers. It lies at the heart of our programme for social and emotional learning in schools and promotes many of the topics covered in *The Teaching Puzzle.*

"Circle Time is such a valuable time. My children learn so much about what it means to be part of a community, and I learn so much about them!"

We work with schools around the country to support their work in this area, and our Classroom Handbooks and other resources offer lesson plans, ideas for activities and guidance for effective sessions.

In school, Circle Time sessions build self-awareness, self-esteem, empathy and a sense of personal empowerment. This encourages positive peer interactions and helps develop children as responsible citizens. The teacher or teaching assistant takes the role of facilitator and the circle establishes equality and a sense of group responsibility based on honesty and trust. Circle Time can be taken as a whole class or in small groups.

Common misconceptions of the Circle Time model include thinking that it is for use only when there is a specific problem to resolve with a specific child (in which case there's a danger it may become like a courtroom hearing) or that encouraging the children to open up and enjoy themselves might make it difficult to maintain the usual discipline. On the contrary, the positive discipline strategies in the Nurturing Programme toolkit are as effective during Circle Time as they are in class and around the school. *Circle Time offers opportunities to develop children's emotional literacy and wellbeing in many ways:*

- Improving their speaking and listening skills
- Extending their powers of concentration
- Enhancing their relationships with each other
- Helping them consider not only how they themselves - *but also others* - feel
- Enabling them to express their views and feelings
- Encouraging them to value and respect each other's differences
- Developing their confidence and self-esteem
- Supporting them as they learn to be kind, not only to each other but also to themselves
- Establishing a sense of community
- Having fun

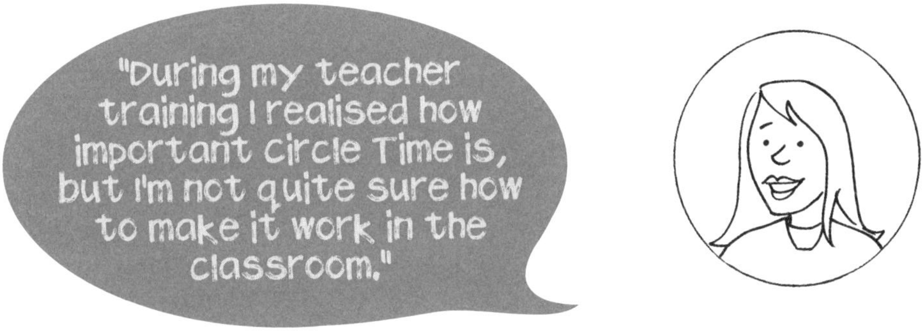

"During my teacher training I realised how important Circle Time is, but I'm not quite sure how to make it work in the classroom."

What makes a successful Circle Time?

A good way to approach Circle Time is to think about how you would like the children to feel during these sessions. We have suggested a few thoughts here:

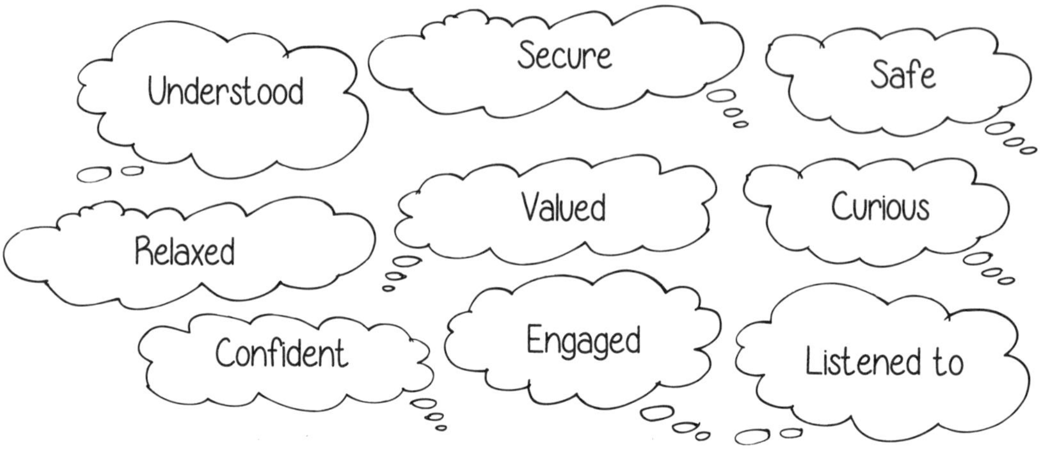

Where to have Circle Time

It's a good idea to keep the location and timetabling of Circle Time the same each week. Keeping this consistent will help the children more easily understand how it works and what is expected of them. Do use the classroom if at all possible, rather than the school hall where it's too big, cold and impersonal. Make space for everyone to sit comfortably in a circle and check it's free from noise and distractions. Some people have a special shared space always kept free for Circle Time. The important thing is that the children feel that they can claim that space as theirs. You could put a note on the door asking *Please do not disturb us during our Circle Time*. Circle Time can also be used as a useful tool after a challenging lunch time or incident.

How to plan Circle Time

The Classroom Handbooks for the Early Years Foundation Stage, Key Stage 1 and Key Stage 2 offer everything you need to plan for Circle Time, from background information, reward system ideas and relevant story books to a scheme of work with detailed session plans for every age group.

The first step for very young children in the Foundation Stage is to offer short, frequent and regular experiences of gathering together in a circle, e.g., at snack time, story time and for games. At Key Stages 1 and 2, older children will enjoy practising Circle Time games as warm-up activities in PE and will relish the sessions suggested in our Key Stage 1 and Key Stage 2 Classroom Handbooks, whether you go for three 15-minute sessions a week or one 45-minute session that they can really get their teeth into.

Getting started

It is useful to gather together a few special items to use in Circle Time. These could be placed in an eyecatching bag or basket that you can hold up at the beginning of the session to make it clear that Circle Time is different from any other time of the week, with unusual and intriguing resources to use and enjoy.

We recommend that you include:

- A talking object such as a ball or small toy; when the ball is gently rolled or passed between the children, it shows whose turn it is to speak
- Age-appropriate puppets or soft toys for performing simple roleplays
- Any equipment you need for games and workbreaks
- A collaborative reward system, e.g., a bag of glass gems and a clear plastic pot to collect them in (see Chapter 3 for more ideas)
- An attention grabber to bring children back together after any activities that require them to break up the circle

It's important to gather the children into a circle, with both you and them sitting at the same level, on chairs or on the floor. Welcome them warmly and explain what is going to happen. You could start by saying, *"Everyone is going to have the chance to get to know each other better, have fun together and talk things through."*

Establishing the agreements in Circle Time

To make Circle Time feel safe, it's essential to start with a set of agreements that apply to Circle Time. These are repeated each week, and once the children are familiar with them, they can remind you and each other what they are. They might for instance include the following:

- We take turns to talk by passing the ball to show whose turn it is
- We can 'pass' if we don't want to say anything
- We earn gems by listening to each other
- Anything private we say in the circle stays in the circle unless I think a child may not be safe, in which case I'd need to tell X so they can help

It won't be long before you have set up your own routine and built your own ideas into your Circle Time sessions, but we've put a few thoughts to help get you started in the checklist below.

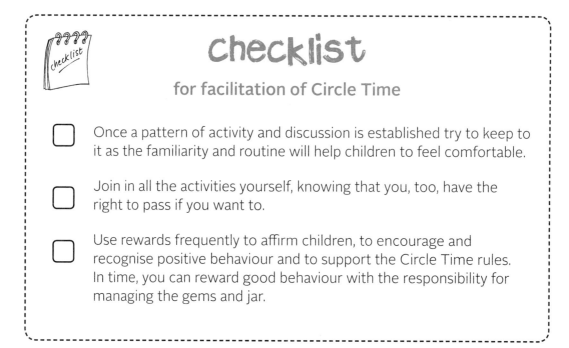

Checklist

for facilitation of Circle Time

- [ ] Once a pattern of activity and discussion is established try to keep to it as the familiarity and routine will help children to feel comfortable.
- [ ] Join in all the activities yourself, knowing that you, too, have the right to pass if you want to.
- [ ] Use rewards frequently to affirm children, to encourage and recognise positive behaviour and to support the Circle Time rules. In time, you can reward good behaviour with the responsibility for managing the gems and jar.

- [ ] Manage low-level disruptive behaviour by keeping your focus on what's going well, remembering that what we pay attention to is what we get more of.

- [ ] Make sure you have some games and workbreak activities up your sleeve to bring the class together, to complement the week's theme and to keep things light-hearted and fun. If the games are quick and lively they will vary the pace of the session, help the group to keep their focus.

- [ ] If you are writing up children's comments on a board or flipchart, remember to include everyone's ideas, even if you don't agree with them. You can always follow up with a group discussion to tease out an issue surrounding these comments.

- [ ] It is very unlikely that the whole class will feel the same thing, or react in the same way. Keep opening up the conversation to include different views.

- [ ] We can be quick to want to get to the root of a problem, but asking *"why?"* is not usually helpful, and can leave children feeling confused and powerless if they do not know the reason. Instead, try reflecting the issue back to the child or ask them to tell you more about what else they were feeling or doing at the time.

- [ ] Remember that some children will take time before they will want to contribute to the discussion and that silent reflection can be as powerful as active participation.

- [ ] Try using empathic phrases that summarise and reflect back any issues that are raised by the group such as *"It sounds like..."*, *"What I'm hearing is..."* This helps the group to understand what the issue is and to feel that they are able to offer a response themselves.

Empathy in Circle Time

Try not to be tempted to use 'quick fix' responses during Circle Time. *If, for example, a child tells the class that they are feeling sad because:*

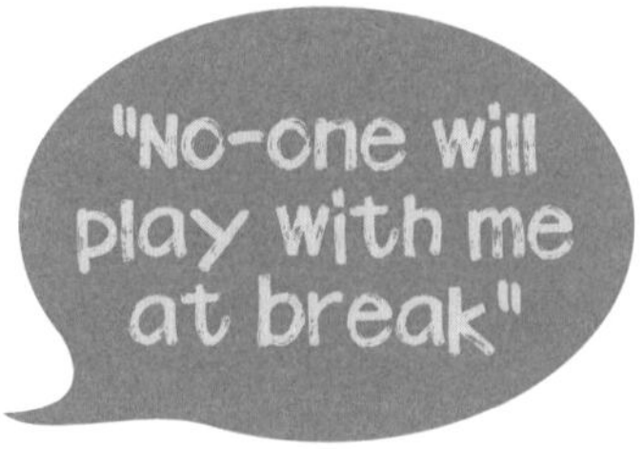

"No-one will play with me at break"

We can then respond empathically in the session rather than offer ideas or advice. We could use this opportunity to expand that child's emotional vocabulary and to help them to express themself more fully.

You could respond:

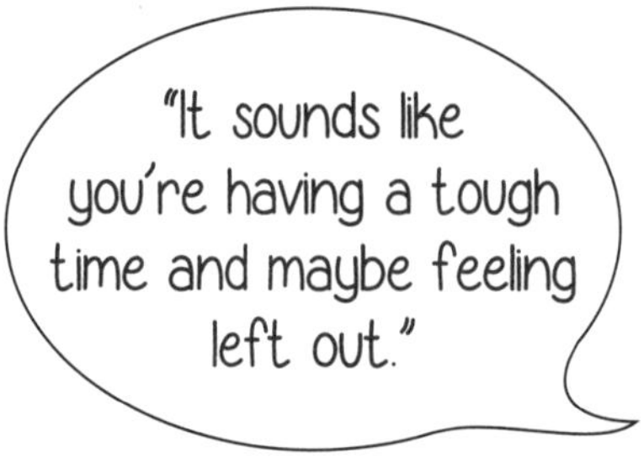

"It sounds like you're having a tough time and maybe feeling left out."

Empathy is our ace card

This might describe their feelings and leave it open for them to end the conversation there or to share more with the group about what is going on.

Facilitation

When leading a group, the success of the session depends a lot on the facilitator being positive and giving plenty of praise and encouragement.

Essential facilitation skills

- Warmth, enthusiasm and humour
- Respect, empathy and a nurturing attitude towards yourself and others
- Welcoming and open body language
- Allowing children the right to pass
- Clear boundaries with flexibility
- Clarity and organisation
- Self-awareness
- Active listening
- Active ignoring

Extra notes

The relevance of meeting children's emotional needs

We can sometimes feel concerned about handling sensitive emotional issues. On the whole, children tend to be sensitive to adult's confidence levels and will adjust their own openness accordingly. It's not up to the facilitator to solve the problem alone, though they may be the person who initiates getting the help and support that the child needs.

We may worry that Circle Time activities may bring painful feelings or memories to the surface, and it is sometimes hard to resist seeing this as a potential 'can of worms'. It's worth reminding ourselves that the child who discloses such troubles is already living with them whether we know about them or not; they will be influencing the child's ability to learn. These activities simply create a supportive environment within which a suffering child may feel safe enough to begin their healing process.

If a child does disclose abuse of any kind, a sensitive, empathic, emotionally muted response is essential: a highly emotional reaction would be difficult for the child to handle.

Recommended guidelines for responding to disclosure during Circle Time are as follows:

1. I believe you.
2. I'm sorry this has happened to you.
3. It's not your fault.
4. We need to tell X [the designated lead person for safeguarding/child protection] as it's important s/he knows, so we can do our best to keep you safe.

Almost all child sexual abuse – and some physical abuse – is accompanied by the threat of dire consequences if the child tells anyone; this can make disclosure a frightening experience. Within the session, it's important to acknowledge what has been raised, show concern and say that the child will have a chance to talk about it afterwards, without allowing the session to become de-railed.

While Circle Time can be therapeutic, it is not therapy: for the safety of both the disclosing child and the rest of the class, you will want to stay mindful of your responsibility to keep all members of the class safe and of the fact that individual disclosures can be scary for other children to hear.

In essence, the peer group needs to know the disclosure will be followed up without being exposed to the detail.

The Nurturing Programme supports an environment in which children feel able to explore their feelings and to tell the truth about events in their lives. The interests of the child are of paramount importance and should always come first.

Becoming emotionally literate

Here is a wonderful real-life story about a five-year-old boy who had experienced weekly Nurturing Programme Circle Time for three terms. Picture the scene:

The boy's dad is in prison for grievous bodily harm, and his mum is struggling to cope. One day at school, the little boy's behaviour has been extremely challenging all morning. At the end of the morning, he sidles up to the teacher and says,

> "Excuse me, miss. I've been using my personal power to make very poor choices all morning. But you see, my mum shouted at me all the way to school because we were late because I'd watched TV too long and didn't get ready. So my feelings were hurt and I was angry. But I'd like to sit on the Time out cushion now to calm down so I can use my Personal Power to make better choices this afternoon."

This is just one of many accounts that show how a child even that young can master the language and ideas of the Nurturing Programme. Naturally, once explored through Circle Time, the language will filter out into the rest of the school day, the playground and the children's homes.

You can transfer the learning and ideas gained in Circle Time across the whole curriculum. For example, during a lesson on scientific enquiry you could point out how this young person used his Personal Power to persuade others about the benefits of vaccination, or use the language of choices and consequences to discuss environmental change during a geography lesson.

Putting Circle Time into practice

Facilitating Circle Time is a complex skill and takes practice. Do be realistic and stay positive even if your first session doesn't go quite as you had hoped. All of the suggestions outlined in this chapter will come to life when you begin to plan and deliver your Circle Time activities over the term.

Here are summaries of two of the weekly sessions taken from the *Early Years Foundation Stage Handbook* and *Key Stage 2 Classroom Handbook.* These age-appropriate handbooks include detailed session plans and key learning objectives and learning outcomes for each session. The summaries provide an overview of the contents and activities for the different topics but not the detailed weekly session plans; we hope that you will buy the Classroom Handbooks in order to use them for delivering Circle Time in your school (visit centreforemotionalhealth.org.uk to order your copies).

Each session in the Classroom Handbooks – in this case, on Personal Power – starts with an overview:

1. Welcome

A brief round to open the session and re-visit expectations for behaviour during Circle Time, followed by an introduction to – or reminder of – the concept of Personal Power

2. Workbreak

A quick game to change the pace, focus the group and release any restless energy

3. Circle Time forum

Puppets/roleplay or an activity to highlight key issues around topic of the week, followed by time to explore these through discussion and debate

4. Goodbye

An opportunity for the children to offer feedback on their learning and practise simple self-assessment, and a quick round to close the session

Circle Time for different ages

Early Years Foundation Stage: Personal Power

As always, the children and adults sit in a circle and everyone is welcomed to the session. The rules and use of rewards are mentioned. Workbreaks change the pace, encourage everyone's participation and release restless energy.

The topic of Personal Power is introduced using puppets or a story (the Classroom Handbook provides lots of suggestions). Children are invited to respond if they would like to, and the session ends with a song, another game or activity.

Lots of rewards, encouragement and a fun and lively pace help the children to enjoy Circle Time.

Year 5: Personal Power

As always, the children are settled in the circle and the group reviews Circle Time rules, the use of rewards and take part in quick, low-key introductory activity or game. The topic for the session is introduced by saying that it is about how we can all make a difference at school and at home by using our Personal Power (or inner strength) in positive ways, both towards other people and towards ourselves.

An interactive exercise or a pre-rehearsed roleplay (perhaps using puppets) explores how you can use your Personal Power: one example might be to remember to put your completed homework in your bag. This provides a useful starting point for a discussion about positive and negative uses of Personal Power, facilitated by the teacher using ideas detailed in the classroom handbook. These ideas include strategies for managing energy levels, encouraging participation and avoiding disruptive behaviour.

Remember to use a reward system to reinforce desirable behaviour. As with each weekly session, the topic ends with a game and a plenary/goodbye [circle] activity.

Now have a look at the following classroom window and think about it in the light of what we have covered so far in this chapter.

Classroom window

Why is Maya upset? Why is she not joining in the laughter?
What can you do to help?

The backstory

Backstory: Maya is very upset because this is the first time she has asked for the Circle Time talking object to speak. In Circle Time sessions before now she has 'passed'. At the start of this session she felt more confident and decided she would talk about how her teenage brother had upset their mum. When Maya explained that it was because her brother had dyed his hair red everyone laughed, including the teacher.

What you could do to help

It is clear that for Maya this is an issue that is upsetting her. There is conflict at home between her mother and brother. She is feeling worried and scared and is upset when the group laugh; she might not want to speak about it any more. She may regard Circle Time as a place only for jokes and not for feelings. You could respond by reminding children of the Circle Time rules and that it is a place where children and adults listen to each other respectfully. An empathic response to Maya may help her recover, and encourage her to say more – either in the circle or at another time.

Active ignoring

Pay attention to the behaviour that you do want!

We often say to children, *"Just take no notice – you'll only make it worse"* when they are annoyed by the antics of other children in the class. Yet many of us find it hard to take our own good advice when it comes to taking no notice of the trivial, annoying ways children may behave. It's tempting to correct them every time their quirks, irritating minor habits, fidgeting and so on grate on our nerves. But focusing on these minor ways of behaving seldom works, and it can sour the atmosphere between us and the child. There is another way: active ignoring, one of the hardest strategies to use.

Sometimes, people confuse active ignoring with doing nothing. It's worth remembering that this is not the case and that this strategy involves a lot of pro-active decision making. It only works if we can develop the self-control not to react, and to divert our attention away from the behaviour we don't like. But like toothache, once we have noticed something we find annoying, it's quite a challenge to think about anything else!

Children need our attention, and will try to get it in any way they can. If we pay attention to the behaviour we do want, the behaviour we don't want sometimes just goes away. If they know they'll always get our attention when they do something we find annoying, then when they want our attention – hey presto! it's time for that annoying behaviour again.

what we pay attention to is what we get more of

We can't and shouldn't take no notice of potentially dangerous or harmful behaviour – that's different, and needs to be dealt with in one of the ways we have explored in earlier chapters.

What not to ignore

behaviour that risks harm to

people or property

fighting, hitting, etc.

crying because hungry, hurt or frightened

tantrums

obsessional/phobic behaviour

crying because afraid of something real or fantasy

wetting or soiling

head banging

spitting

running off

deliberate damage

angry offensive language

What we might ignore

whining/whingeing/using baby talk

hair-twiddling

fiddling with Velcro on shoes

thumb-sucking

interrupting

nose-picking

*swearing**

*showing off**

telling tales

*calling out**

low-grade rudeness/sullen looks

* Some of these behaviours may need ignoring immediately but should be followed up at an appropriate time, such as asking the child to stay behind when the children are lining up for break. This also sends an important message to the other children.

How we feel / react

If we don't use the strategy of Active Ignoring we can find ourselves responding in a number of ways which can sometimes escalate the situation.

I might...

... get really irritated ... be okay when I'm calm but not when I'm stressed ... answer back in a whiny voice ... bear it for a time, then snap at them ... be anxious about what other people will think ... nag at him till he stops or goes away want to scream ... get sarcastic

Are any of these ways of behaving and our reactions to the behaviour familiar to you? What others are true for you?

Steps for Active Ignoring

1. Be sure about what you want the child to do that would replace the unwanted behaviour
2. Ignore the behaviour for as long as it lasts unless it gets dangerous
3. Do not mention the behaviour directly (e.g. by telling the child you are going to ignore what they are doing, or by asking the child to stop) or indirectly (e.g. by mimicking or criticising)
4. As soon as the unwanted behaviour stops, praise the child - not for stopping what they were doing, but for starting to do what you like (and look out for other opportunities to praise the behaviour you like, too)
5. Ignore the behaviour, not the child as a person. If the behaviour gets worse, it is probably because the child is being ignored altogether, rather than being paid (positive) attention for something other than the unwanted behaviour
6. Think about asking others in the class (e.g. partner, older children) to ignore the behaviour, but without any ganging up or siding with one child against another
7. Think about the reasons behind the behaviour, and what feelings in the child may be triggering it (e.g. upset, frustrated, hungry); if possible, address the problem without drawing attention to the behaviour that has made you aware of it
8. Ask yourself what feelings this annoying behaviour may trigger in yourself, and how you could deal with/recover from/let go of them

Active ignoring in Circle Time

Helpful (Do)

I'm listening to Jake because he is holding the talking ball.

Paying attention to positive behaviour

Unhelpful (Don't)

Don't interrupt!

Paying attention to negative behaviour

Did you know... ?

You can find detailed Circle Time session plans in the Classroom Handbooks. These offer a full scheme of work for PSHE planned for progression from the Foundation Stage through to Year 7.

Each handbook sets out a detailed 10-week rolling programme of Circle Time session plans, together with ideas for consolidating the themes through the rest of the week. The Circle Time session plans are designed for flexible use; they all follow a basic structure that begins with a welcome circle and reminder of group rules and ends with a goodbye circle. Timing can vary to suit the needs of the school and the children. Some schools offer children a weekly 45-minute session throughout Key Stage 2; others break them down to offer three 15-minute sessions a week in the autumn before relaxing into a weekly session during the spring and summer terms; others still offer a weekly 45-minute session in the autumn and then weave other PSHE into their spring and summer plans.

Checklist

for facilitation of Circle Time

- [ ] Think about how you would like the children to feel during Circle Time sessions. Consider your facilitation skills and the ways you help children feel safe and comfortable during Circle Time

- [ ] Prepare your Circle Time resources, remembering the list we suggested on page 159.

- [ ] With a colleague, discuss how you might respond to a disclosure of abuse and ensure that you are up-to-date with your school's safeguarding procedures

- [ ] Think about buying one of the Classroom Handbooks or attending a Centre for Emotional Health workshop

- [ ] Consider offering the parallel 10-week *Nurturing Programme* for parents in your community, and add some of the resources to your staffroom library. For details, please contact Family Links via our website, familylinks.org.uk

- [ ] Think about children who seem particularly withdrawn during Circle Time, or those who are disruptive, and consider how best to meet their needs

- [ ] Try to incorporate some of the key elements and ethos of Circle Time into your regular class lessons

The Staffroom

"Circle Time is a wonderful, safe place for children to express their feelings and understand their peers better."

"I now realise that I was using Circle Time to show the children how annoyed I was with their bad behaviour during the week. They stopped saying anything as they thought I would just get cross."

"We had a fantastic Circle Time session yesterday on Managing Difficult Feelings with Year 6. The class were totally different today much more relaxed!"

"For the first time Maya has been talking to me about what is upsetting her at home. I had no idea that she was so upset about her brother. It's helped me to sort out things to make it better for her."

Chapter 9: Working Effectively with Adults

Tips and strategies for personal and professional relationships

Clear and effective communication is essential in maintaining positive relationships.

In this chapter we will outline some useful communication strategies which are vital in our interactions with adults and children. We need to communicate clearly if we want other people to respect and understand us. We can do this best when we are clear in our own minds about what's going on, and can help others understand our point of view.

This will help us with the people we work and interact with: our colleagues, the children and their parents, inspectors and other agencies. And, of course, our friends and family.

The staffroom climate

Working in a school means building relationships with a number of colleagues and coping with the ups and downs. The important thing is to work towards a positive ethos. Colleague relationships require just as much ongoing attention and investment as relationships formed outside school. Teachers who feel a strong, positive connection to their pupils *and* to their colleagues are likely to be more effective in the classroom and stay in the teaching profession longer.

Teaching can be very unpredictable and tiring. We may not always get it right. We may be faced with complex and difficult situations. An emotionally healthy school is one where individuals are able to express their frustrations or doubts without feeling judged or criticised.

> "When I first started my job, I felt more anxious about going into the staffroom at breaktimes than about my class."

For many schools, the sense of mutual support among colleagues can be a key factor in it's overall wellbeing and success The Nurturing Programme approaches working with colleagues in much the same way as it does working with children. Building our emotional intelligence is a lifelong pursuit.

Many of the ideas we introduced in Chapter 1 of this book could equally be applied to the staffroom environment. If there was a weather chart on the wall, what would it read? Staffrooms can be tricky to negotiate, especially for new or trainee teachers. Often there is a very supportive and nurturing group of colleagues who have welcomed you into the fold, but sometimes the climate in staffrooms can leave staff feeling unsupported and un-nurtured.

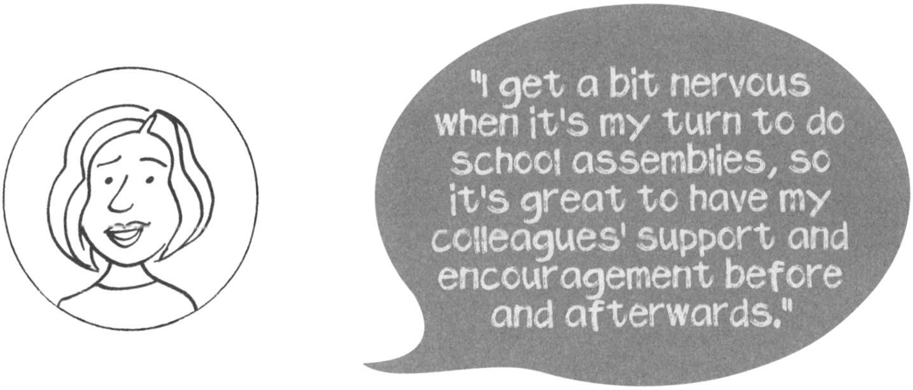

"I get a bit nervous when it's my turn to do school assemblies, so it's great to have my colleagues' support and encouragement before and afterwards."

It's not just our colleagues who can pose a challenge sometimes, because partnership with parents and carers takes work too.

We know that a key success factor for a child is when a school works in partnership with parents and carers. At its best, this is consistent, mutually-supportive and energising. Sometimes, though, it can be challenging to make this partnership work effectively. There can be different views, poor communication and even judgement and criticism.

One way to manage an awkward situation at work, with colleagues or parents, is to communicate clearly and positively so that they will respect you and understand your needs. It's also really helpful to remember to communicate your successes and appreciation as often as you can. One useful technique is to use "I" statements, which we will come to shortly. First of all it's worth identifying how we react when challenged by another adult.

How do I respond when feeling challenged?

Let's think about how we respond when someone challenges or confronts us. Often it's in one of four ways:

Responses to Challenges

submissive	**passive aggressive**	**aggressive**	**assertive**
↓	↓	↓	↓
yielding	manipulative	blaming "You" messages	"I" statements
↓	↓	↓	↓
powerless resentful	power struggle	power struggle	power retained
increased stress	increased stress	increased stress	decreased stress

When we are assertive, it's like being balanced on a seesaw. We keep our sense of power and the other person does too. We each respect the other's point of view and we manage to resolve the issue. It's what is often known as a win-win situation: we both feel okay afterwards and the relationship becomes stronger. This is the ideal way to respond.

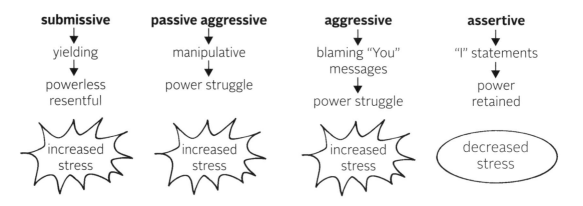

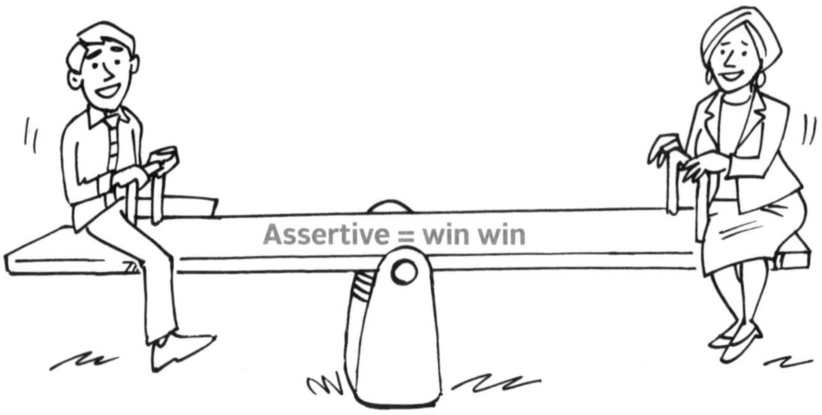

Being submissive, passive aggressive or aggressive usually unbalances the seesaw of a relationship. If we give in when we don't want to, we may wake up in the middle of the night and find we're angry or miserable. We may get pushed around another time – or take it out on someone weaker. If we respond aggressively, the problem usually escalates unless the other person becomes submissive, in which case we may feel we've 'won'. But the other person will feel worse, and our relationship with them will worsen too.

We might always respond in the same way, but usually what happens is that our reaction depends on the power relationship between the other person and ourselves. Some people are submissive with those in authority (like a boss), and aggressive towards those with less power than themselves (like children). Others become aggressive when confronted by an authority figure, and are calmly assertive in other situations. Most of us use a mixture of all three responses depending on our mood and that of the other person. There can also be a knock-on effect whereby one type of response leads to another. For instance, if an inexperienced teacher is confronted by the headteacher or a member of the senior management team, they might be submissive because they feel at the bottom of the pecking order. This could impact their own emotional health and affect the climate of the classroom.

Let's have a look at some examples of how and why we might respond in these different ways. We might be submissive when responding to a parent who barges into the classroom in the middle of a lesson to complain about how the school is managing her child's behaviour: *'I'm so sorry that your child doesn't like Time Out to Calm Down. We'll change how we manage this situation."*

When asked by the headteacher to do playground duty to cover someone who is off sick, we might respond passive-aggressively by saying to the headteacher's face, "*Yes, of course,*" and then to colleagues "*She has no idea how busy I am – she could do it herself sometimes.*" Or we might respond aggressively by saying angrily to the headteacher, "*I don't see why it's got to be me. I'm really busy and it's unfair that you don't ask a more senior member of staff to stand in.*"

Using "I" statements to be assertive

We can avoid unhelpful responses to challenge by using an "I" statement to help us stay assertive and to find a way of balancing the seesaw of our relationships. "I" statements give us a way of talking about – and taking responsibility for – difficult situations, thoughts and feelings. Although this may feel risky, it increases our chances of being understood, and reduces the number of destructive arguments we might have. By turning our response around so that we are not blaming the recipient, we respect the other person's point of view, whilst maintaining our own boundaries and staying true to ourselves. We still can't be sure that the other person will respond the way we'd like them to, but it's more likely than if we sulk, moan or lose our temper.

Let's have a look at how we can turn a **blaming "You" message** *into a more* **helpful and assertive "I" statement.** *Perhaps a colleague has started discussing a child's family situation in the staffroom when it is full of staff and visitors:*

"Why do you all make me join in staffroom chat about troubled children or parents?"

"I feel uncomfortable when troubled children and parents are discussed in the staffroom. If I am involved in the discussion I'd feel more comfortable for it to be in a small, discreet group."

Here's an example of Mrs Khan struggling with not being able to relax at breaktimes.

"You" message (unhelpful):

> "You stress me out talking about work all through break when what I really need is a breather from my class."

An assertive "I" statement (helpful):

> "I feel less ready for my next session when we talk about work all through break. Let's talk about life outside work, too."

"I" statements allow us to say how we are feeling, why it matters to us and how we would like the issue dealt with. Let's look again at the example of a parent who raises concerns about how the school is managing their child's behaviour. If we feel challenged or criticised by their approach, we could say:

"I feel it is important for us to find agreement on this situation because then we can work in partnership. What I'd like is for us to arrange a meeting when we can discuss this in depth."

If the parent interrupts you in the middle of teaching (as in the example described on page 182), try explaining that you need to carry on teaching so perhaps they could meet with you to talk it through at hometime.

Here's another example of the "I" statement being used successfully by Mr George in conversation with Mrs Wilson:

> "I feel overloaded when I'm asked to do extra duties because, being new to teaching, I'm finding it hard to keep up with preparation. What I'd like is to be asked once I'm managing my workload better."

Checklist

for using "I" statements successfully

- [ ] Say how you feel, using words that describe your emotions.
- [ ] Describe the situation without blaming or criticising the person involved; avoiding the word "you" keeps the description general, which is easier for the other person to hear.
- [ ] Be clear about why this is a problem for you and what need isn't being met.
- [ ] Think about what might help to solve the problem, from your point of view.
- [ ] If you'd like to have a go, you can think of a situation where you may have responded with submission or aggression. You can copy the form on the next page onto a sheet of paper and fill it in with ideas for how you might respond in the future.

Giving an "I" Statement

I feel *(say how you feel)* ....

When *(describe the situation and avoid using 'you')* ....

....

Because *(state your need that is not being met and why it matters)*

....

What I'd like is *(describe what would help you to meet your need)*

....

....

Did you know... ?

There's a matching 10-week Family Links Nurturing Programme for parents!

The Family Links Nurturing Programme for parents offers a parallel model for emotionally healthy families. Many schools offer parent groups to their local community to match the ethos, strategies and approach that they are using with the Nurturing Programme in school. If parents, children and staff are all learning and using the same language and strategies, the child benefits from this really consistent approach.

"I" statements are also a great way to show others that we appreciate and value their views, opinions and efforts.

"I feel so delighted when I see responsible behaviour because it shows me how well this class can work together. I'm looking forward to seeing more of this in the next activity."

(to Jake's Mum):
"I am really pleased that we've agreed how to manage Jake's homework because it makes it much easier when we are both giving him the same message and I know he finds it helpful too. It would be great to see if there are any other areas we could discuss to help Jake do even better."

Problem solving

Another strategy we can use when we are working with colleagues, parents or other adults is problem-solving. Everyone needs to know how to make decisions, how to solve problems, and how to negotiate. It doesn't matter what job we do or what our role is: whatever life we lead, these are useful skills. They help us find a way to sort out difficulties and disagreements and reach solutions.

Learning and using these skills lowers tension and reduces head-on conflicts. What often happens when two people have different ideas on something is a stalemate or a conflict is that both people want to win the argument, so become deaf to each other's point of view. The ways we respond to challenge come in again here: if we can be assertive and respectful, and if the other person can do this too, we're more likely to solve the problem. The hard part is to think clearly; never an easy thing to do when we're in the grip of strong emotions.

So we're going to look at ways of working out solutions to tricky situations. Having a clear set of steps to follow can help to keep us thinking clearly, focusing on finding a solution rather than blaming someone else for creating the problem in the first place.

Here is an example of how problem solving might work in practice. Most school staff can identify with the problem of getting children settled and calm in class after lunchtime break.

Steps for Problem Solving

1. Work out exactly what the problem is

2. Be clear about whose problem it is (sometimes what may be a problem for you is not causing a problem for someone else)

3. Discuss what has already been tried to deal with the problem; try to avoid blame and fault-finding

4. Consider what would solve the problem and what the goal is; make it reasonable and achievable

5. Think of as many ways as possible to reach the goal; welcome all ideas at this stage

6. Decide which solutions to try and have a go at

7. If the problem remains, go back to the list, check steps 1 and 4 again and then try out some other ideas

How parents and teachers can work together

A great way for teachers and parents to collaborate about individual children is to do the quiz (see page 150) together. They could discuss with the child what they think he/she is capable of doing and would like to do more of. Then they could compare the lists so that everyone understands the child's developmental needs and capabilities, ensuring that, together, you have appropriate expectations of the child, both at home and at school.

The purpose of this exercise is to identify the capabilities of each child and check whether the child is being controlled or empowered (see page 143 for more on this).

Why not try it out with three or four parents after school one day?

It's useful and fun and might lead on to further discussion that will make parents feel more involved in their child's life at school.

For example:

What can I do?

Pack my own lunchbox

Make sure my pencil case is in order

What do I think I can do more of?

Getting my school uniform ready the night before

If the school expects a child in Reception to get dressed independently after PE, do parents also have the same expectation of their five-year-old getting dressed at home?

If any issues arise from conflicting expectations between a parent and the school, this gives you the perfect opportunity to have a conversation and start to work in partnership to help a child to become more independent.

Similarly, at school you could make a list of activities and discuss these with the parent, along with their home list. It's a great way for the child to be able to connect their home and school life, and to show how parents and teachers can work together to ensure healthy development. More in Chapter 9.

In order to help children develop in every way – physically, mentally, intellectually, socially and emotionally – it's often best as parents and school staff to follow rather than to lead children. If you offer them different activities they will soon guide you as to which ones they enjoy and which ones offer the right challenges. As children get older they are more able to express what they want to do and they have stronger opinions about it too. Their peer group and popular culture will increasingly have an influence.

Children have a great need to play: it's how they learn. They are explorers, scientists and artists. If we offer them activities both in the home and at school that are right for their age and stage of development, we will meet their needs and meet our needs too. For example, a happily occupied child is unlikely to whinge or whine!

School and home are the two most important influences in a child's life, so it's very important to make sure that these two areas can work together to be of mutual benefit. *For instance:*

- If a child has fun playing active games and running around in the playground or park they are less likely to run riot at home.
- If a child learns to handle food or cook at home or at school they are less likely to be fussy about their food.
- If the child's teachers and parents encourage a child to talk and really listen to them, that child is likely to be less demanding of attention.

All the way through their childhood and adolescence, children need us to give them new experiences that are right for their age. Understanding developmental milestones and age-appropriate activities is of huge benefit to both parents and teachers so that they know *what* to expect and *when* to expect it.

Children also need us to take an interest in what they are interested in, and introduce them to the things we enjoy. If we can enjoy a child's learning while they are young, we'll help them want to go on exploring and learning new things all their lives.

working effectively with parents

We've already discussed how helpful clear communication is when we are working in partnership with parents. The strategies of "I" statements and problem solving may offer us some ideas for dealing with challenges. There are also lots of different ways that schools use to work effectively with parents, in particular, by:

- Making sure that the school is as welcoming and inclusive as possible; staff working in administrative and school office areas are a really important part in creating and maintaining the atmosphere and exterior of a warm and welcoming school

- Keeping updated displays of work and information in the entrance hall; you might want to have your whole-school collaborative reward system on display

- Sending messages home to make sure parents and carers know when their child has received an award or a star of the week in assembly Pointing out good conduct as well as alerting them to negative behaviour

- Thinking how classroom projects might benefit from the input of parents, e.g., the Feelings Wall (see Chapter 3, page 62). Inviting them in to talk about their work, their culture or to introduce the class to a new baby in their family

- Finding ways of using the skills of the parents to help you, e.g., in the class or in the garden

Problem solving with colleagues

There might be some particular problems you are trying to solve at the moment, so you could have a go at thinking one through using the form below to guide you. We've put in an example scenario and possible responses to give you the idea. Choose something manageable to begin with – not the most difficult thing you've ever had to confront!

What exactly is the problem?

Staff feeling resentful at having to take on playground duty last minute when a colleague is off sick.

Whose problem is it?

The staff

What has already been tried?

Headteacher approaching staff to cover at random.

What is the goal; what would solve the problem?

Reduce staff resentment, responsibilities shared in a fair way.

Ways to reach the goal:

Draw up a procedure to follow. Discuss possible solutions at staff meeting, draw up a rota, circulate possible rota.

What to try:

Agree at staff meeting what to try first.

The Staffroom

"Circle Time is a wonderful, safe place for children to express their feelings and understand their peers better."

"I now realise that I was using Circle Time to show the children how annoyed I was with their bad behaviour during the week. They stopped saying anything as they thought I would just get cross."

"We had a fantastic Circle Time session yesterday on Managing Difficult Feelings with Year 6. The class were totally different today much more relaxed!"

"For the first time Maya has been talking to me about what is upsetting her at home. I had no idea that she was so upset about her brother. It's helped me to sort out things to make it better for her."

Extra notes on Chapter 9

Chapter 10: Continuing our Professional Journey

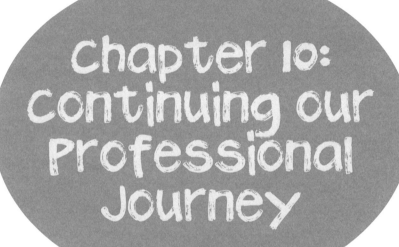

Are the puzzle pieces fitting together?

How to consolidate everything you have learnt so far and prepare to continue your professional journey

If you have got this far, you will have covered many of the key ideas that the Nurturing Programme promotes and have hopefully tried out some of our practical exercises in the classroom.

We know that working in schools and doing the best job possible for the children in your care can be a puzzle at times. We hope you have found this book a useful companion and guide as you have gone about putting some of the puzzle pieces together. This is the chance to take stock and reflect on the journey so far.

Have a go at filling in the self-evaluation to record some thoughts about your progress. You'll notice that we've included a slot for comments from the children you work with. Children are very perceptive, and can come up with shrewd observations!

Self-evaluation

How am I changing?

How do I think my classroom or the school environment that I work in is changing?

What ideas and strategies am I using confidently?

Which ideas and strategies am I less sure about?

Do I ask the children I work with, "What makes our classroom a happy learning place?", "What gets in the way of our learning?"

What is the emotional climate like in my classroom or workplace at the moment?

What's next?

Here's another chance to reflect. Remember how you were at the beginning of this book and think about how far you have come. You might like also like to think about where you'd like to go from here.

What sort of teacher/staff member am I now?

Where do I want to be in a year's time?

What are my aims/goals for the next five years of my career?

School Holiday
SCHOOL BUS
THE RIGHT TRACK
checklist
Teaching Puzzle
DOs
DON'Ts
I'm glad to be me
I'm proud of myself
circle time
School
Home
THE RIGHT TRACK
SCHOOL BUS
Nurturing Ourselves
Teaching Puzzle
STRESS
SCHOOL BUS
YOU ARE HERE
THE RIGHT TRACK
SCHOOL BUS
SCHOOL BUS
Teaching Puzzle

The Nurturing Toolbox

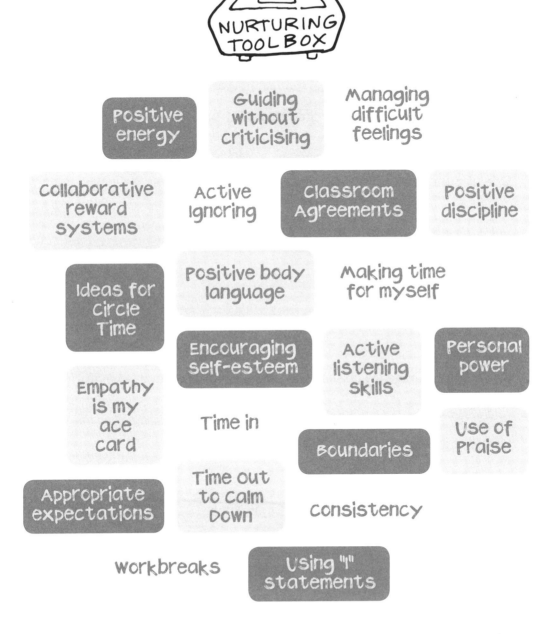

- Positive energy
- Guiding without criticising
- Managing difficult feelings
- Collaborative reward systems
- Active Ignoring
- Classroom Agreements
- Positive discipline
- Ideas for Circle Time
- Positive body language
- Making time for myself
- Encouraging self-esteem
- Active listening skills
- Personal power
- Empathy is my ace card
- Time in
- Boundaries
- Use of Praise
- Appropriate expectations
- Time out to Calm Down
- Consistency
- Workbreaks
- Using "I" statements

As we come towards the end of this book, it's worth remembering what 'tools' you have gathered to keep in your personal toolbox. It should be pretty full!

How far have I come?

Here's a way of revisiting some of the ideas and teaching methods we have explored. As you work your way through the list completing the statements, make a note of how far you have come and what still needs more time and effort. You might find that you have forgotten about some of the topics and need to look back at previous chapters to remind yourself what to do.

One positive thing I said to a child this week was:

....

One of our classroom agreements is:

....

When did I last reward a child?

....

When did I last collectively reward the class?

....

How do I encourage my class to use their Personal Power in a helpful way?

....

One way of helping a child's self-esteem is to:

....

Three activities I have planned for Circle Time:

....

....

....

....

Three ideas for workbreaks are:

One reason I'm proud of myself today is:

If a child is very critical of others, they might be feeling:

One way I calm down when I am angry is:

An "I" statement I recently made was:

One label I have realised I am putting on a child is:

Three ways I manage difficult feelings in the classroom are:

One example of a choice and consequence that works well at school is:

One way I nurture myself is:

Where we are now
(how far I've come and what I've learnt)

Better at teamwork

More empathic

Taking care of myself

Listening more skillfully

More in charge

Appropriate expectations

Sensitively facilitating fun Circle Times

Clear boundaries and agreements

Positive discipline

More confident

Calm

Guiding without criticising

Managing difficult feelings

Using "I" statements

Stronger self-esteem

Where I'd like to finish
(extra skills I'd like to gain in my career)

More confidence

Innovative teaching

Happy classes year after year

More energy

Understanding and respect

More responsibility

Taking on more extra-curricular activities

A lifelong love of teaching

Being a role-model who makes a big difference to the lives of many children

Valuing myself

More empathy

The nurturing toolbox will help the children to:

Feel good about themselves

Feel part of a strong community

Listen to each other

Show empathy

Be positive and assertive

Manage and communicate their feelings constructively

Make friends

Be honest

Be confident

Be accepting of others

Become responsible citizens

Have self-control

Become thoughtful and resilient adults

Early warnings
(signs of stress in adults)

Impatience

Exhaustion

Anger

Shouting in class

Not sleeping

Tearful

Anxiety

Loss of appetite

Feeling of being overwhelmed

No interest in work

Depression

Early warnings
(signs of stress in children)

Defiance

Shouting

Agression

Resistance to discipline

No interest in schoolwork

Tiredness

Loss of appetite

Stomach ache

Lying

Lacklustre attitude

Bouts of crying

Short fused

Argumentative

Bullying / bullied

Poor social skills

Signposts
(on the right track in the classroom)

Enthusiastic and cooperative children

Laughter and fun

Good listening skills

Caring and empathy displayed by class

Exciting learning opportunities

Praising and receiving praise

Enjoying the company of the class

Looking forward to each day

More energy

Positive attitude

Problem solving

Self-nurturing

Feeling valued and respected

Able to cope effectively with daily demands and workload

Looking forward to new opportunities

Flexibility

Major hazards
(extra stressful situations)

Bullying

Redundancy

Changing job

Bereavement

Divorce

Moving House

Illness

Financial worries

Difficulties with colleagues

Difficulties with parents

Ofsted inspection

Children who need extra support

Children who are coping with bereavement or trauma

Fighting

Injury in class

Extra-curriculum responsibilities

Staff meetings

Assemblies

School productions

Building work

In case of breakdown
(emergency survival kit)

Talk to colleagues and compare notes

Make sure you have time for yourself every day

Carefully plan your weekends to include something nurturing

Exercise

Ask for help from colleagues or more senior staff

Think before acting

Put yourself in the shoes of the children

Make the most of opportunities for in-service training

Do creative activities to inspire you with ideas for teaching

Problem solve

Manage your time effectively

Make your classroom or working environment an attractive, welcoming place to work

Breathe deeply

Use relaxation exercises

Look back over *The Teaching Puzzle* to remind yourself of useful positive strategies

Keeping my life in balance

Which of the things in the weights on the opposite page are most important to you? Label the weights below with the ideas you feel most strongly about and of course add any extra ones of your own.

The more you can invest in yourself the sooner the children will be able to benefit. It doesn't matter if you can't do many of the things every day, as you will inevitably have bad days and difficult times just like everyone else, but at least when that happens you will have enough to draw on. And on good days you will be an important role model for the children.

Emotional investment in your school

The nurturing toolbox is a reminder of the different ways we can encourage cooperative behaviour in the children we work with, and maintain a happy, calm and healthy classroom climate.

It's vitally important to look after yourself. If you are stressed and unhappy at school, you won't be able to give anything to the children or to your colleagues. The weights below are some of the things you can do to create an emotionally healthy classroom, and some things you can do to nurture yourself.

If we always do what we've always done, we'll always get what we've always got!
Empathy is your ace card

The Staffroom

"My aim is to introduce ideas from the Nurturing Programme into all aspects of school life. I am amazed at the impact simple techniques have had on the children and the staff!"

"I feel really supported by all these new ideas. I love that all the school staff help each other remember and practise what we've learnt in a consistent whole-school way."

"I've been teaching for a long time, and I take all these ideas very seriously in my practice. It's nice to see so many of my own strategies in this book and discover ways to fine-tune them."

"Teaching is so much better - I'm determined to hold onto everything I've learnt. I actually look forward to coming into school now."

continuing the journey

So here we are at the end of the book. We hope that you will feel better equipped to enjoy life as an adult working with children in school. It can be a wonderful job and you now have *The Teaching Puzzle* as a guide to help you **Aspire, Flourish and Achieve!**

Recommended workbreaks

These quick games, taken from the Classroom Handbooks, can make effective workbreaks in the classroom. It is useful for teaching and non-teaching staff to familiarise themselves with a 'bank' of these in order to be able to choose an appropriate one on the spur of the moment. If pupils are excitable or agitated, a relaxation exercise can provide a calming workbreak; if they are lethargic, restless or losing concentration, an energising game can change the pace and help pupils re-focus with new enthusiasm on the task in hand. We've indicated games that are medium/longer in length and those used specifically for relaxation purposes.

1, 2, 3, Swap

The facilitator points at two children, saying "X and Y, 1, 2, 3 swap!", at which pointthey exchange places as quickly as possible to earn a gem each for the group reward jar.

Alliteration Affirmation

The group stands in a circle and everyone takes turns to say his/her name, preceding it with a positive adjective about him/herself (e.g. Cool Charlie, Intelligent Ibrahim, Amazing Amelia, etc.)

Alphabet Circle [medium]

The children line up in a circle in alphabetical order, by the initials of their first names, then move randomly around the room before returning to stand in the same position at a signal from you. Repeat until this is down to a fine art and make the point that 'practice makes perfect'. An alternative is to use surnames.

Back to Back

Divide into pairs and sit back to back on the floor, then try to get to a standing position without using hands – just using each other's backs for support.

Balloons

The group sits in a circle and bats five balloons in the air, making sure these stay in the air and don't touch the floor (or they are 'out'). The game's over when all five balloons are 'out'.

Birthday Bonanza

The children move around the room with everyone chanting the month of their birthday, very quietly at first but getting louder until those with a month in common find each other. They then need to order themselves by date, before coming together with the rest of the class in a whole class birthday circle. To finish, everyone in turn calls out his/her date/month of birth, starting with "1st January!".

Buzz Timestable

The children take turns to count, replacing multiples of a given number (e.g. '3')with the word "buzz" (e.g. "1", "2", "buzz", "4", "5", "buzz", etc). Repeat as often as time allows, using different numbers each time.

Cannonballs [longer]

The class kneels in two rows, facing each other. Each row, or team, creates roughly equal quantities of scrunched-up newspaper 'cannonballs' and keeps them to hand on the floor. On the count of three, both teams hurl their cannonballs at the opposing team, aiming to get them behind their opponents. Both teams use not only their own cannonballs but also those that fall in front of them. The game ends when the adult judges that sufficient energy has been expended.

Carwash

The class stands in two rows, facing each other like the brushes in a carwash. They take turns to be the 'car', walking down between the lines and receiving pats on the back/applause/compliments/cheers.

Changing Places

Introduce this game by explaining that if what you say is true for a child, s/he will need to get up and change places with someone else for whom it is also true. Give several examples – you can choose statements particularly relevant to your class - until all the children have moved around, eg "Change places if... you like ice cream/have a brother or sister/have a pet at home/are wearing something blue/enjoy football", etc.

Clap, Bob, Coffee

In pairs face each other.

First person says "one", other person says "two", first person says "three", and repeat (which brings it back to the first person). For the next round, start by clapping hands, "two", "three" and repeat. Next replace "two" with a bob and repeat.

Finally instead of saying "three" replace by saying "coffee" and repeat. So that the final round is *clap hands*, bob, "coffee"!

Colour Stamp

The caller calls out a colour and the children stamp around the room to touch something of that colour. The game may be played until a number of colours have been called out.

Countdown

The class sits wherever is convenient. The aim is to count down from the total number of people in the class (children and adults) to zero, and then to lift off (by standing up and cheering). Each person may call out only one number, in descending order, and if two or more people say the same number the game starts again from the beginning.

Daisy Chain

The children stand in a circle. The caller calls out numbers and the children move freely in the room to link arms in groups of that number. Repeat as often as time allows.

Duck Duck Goose

The group sits in a circle while one child walks around the outside of the circle, gently tapping each person and saying "duck". They choose one person to be called "goose". They then try to go around the outside of the circle and sit in the spare place (where the "goose" had been sitting) before the "goose" catches them.

Earthquake

The class forms equal numbers of 'houses' (two people with their arms in the air and hands touching to make the roof) and 'people' (individuals – one to each house). When you call out 'houses', all those being houses let go of each other and make new houses (with new partners). When you call out "People", all those being people move to a new house. When you call out "Earthquake", everyone moves.

Eight Legs

The class sits in a circle with legs outstretched. The person who starts the game lifts his or her feet one at a time, counting, "One, two". The next person counts "Three, four" as s/he lifts her feet and so on around the circle. The eighth leg to be counted is 'out' – tucked back and not counted again. The next person starts again at one and again the eighth leg is 'out'. The game continues until only one leg is left. This can also be played as a competitive team game with equal-sized teams sitting around their tables.

Electric Zoom

The group stands in a circle (like an electric circuit). The words "zoom, zoom" are quickly passed around the circle (like an electric current). If anyone says "zoom turn" the zoom changes direction. If anyone says "power cut", everyone moves to a new place in the circle (the circuit breaks). The last person to speak then becomes the first to start a new "zoom, zoom" on its journey. Everyone has one chance to say "zoom turn" or "power cut"; when they have used it, they sit down and continue to participate in the zooms.

Eleven

The class stands in a circle and a volunteer counts out loud, starting with '1' and counting no further than '3'. The next person follows on, starting with the next number and counting up – again between one and three numbers. When '11' is reached, the person who says it is 'out' and sits down. The next person begins again with '1'. The last to remain standing is the winner.

Give yourself a Hug (relaxation)

Suggest the children could give themselves a hug by wrapping their arms around their shoulders and gently squeezing

Group Juggle

The children stand in a circle, facing inwards. One person starts with the ball and chooses one person to throw it to. Remind them to say the name of the person before they throw it. That person now repeats with a different person. Ask the children to keep their hands in front of them until they have received the ball/beanbag and passed it on; then they put their hands behind them to show that they have had their turn. Once everyone has had their turn, repeat, emphasising that the same people will throw to/receive from each other every time. Add more balls/bean bags to increase difficulty.

Heads or Tails?

Ask the group to stand make a circle. Show them a coin and explain that they need to predict if the coin will land heads or tails once it is flipped. To indicate their prediction they either place both hands on their head (heads) or both hands behind them (tails).

Flip the coin.

If they predicted correctly they can remain standing. Repeat the process until there is only one winner.

Focused Relaxation [relaxation]

The class sits in a circle and relaxes for a few minutes by gazing at a flower or ornament in the centre of the circle and encourage everyone to focus on it quietly.

The Key to my Heart

The children sit in a circle and pass a key around to music; when the music stops, the child with the key says, "The key to my heart is..." and names one of his/her favourite things (e.g. swimming, chocolate ice cream, Harry Potter books, etc.)

Repeat as often as time allows.

March to my Beat

The children march around the classroom in time to the beat maintained by a volunteer, using a tambourine, a drum or clapping. The pace of marching needs to reflect variations in the beat.

Music Relaxation (relaxation)

The class sits on chairs in a circle, or on the floor, preferably with hands resting in laps and eyes closed or looking downwards. Whilst playing quiet, soothing music encourage the children to focus quietly on their breathing, gradually making it soft and slow.

Over and Under

The class stands in two or more parallel lines with legs apart. The children passing a ball back alternatively over their head or between their legs. When it reaches the person at the back they run to the front of the line. Repeat until the original leader is at the front again.

Pass the Ball

The class sits in a circle with outstretched legs. Place a ball on the legs of one member of the group, who then tips the ball gently onto the legs of a neighbour, using legs only. The aim is to get the ball back to the first player without it touching the floor.

Pass the Bell

The class stands (or sits) in a circle and passes a small handbell from person to person, focusing on not letting it ring.

Pass the Marker [longer]

The class divides into equal-sized small groups. Each group has a marker pen, which passes around the group from hand to hand (not just each person). When the marker reaches the hand it started from, the group gives a silent cheer (everyone raising their arms). The first group to give a silent cheer is the winner.

Pat the Dog

The children stand in a circle with their hands resting lightly on their neighbours' backs and pass a pat on the shoulder around the circle as quickly as possible; a double-pat has the power to change the direction in which the pat is travelling.

Popcorn

Everyone in the class bounces up and down. If someone bumps (gently!) into someone else, they link arms and bounce together – sticking together like sticky popcorn. The pairs then become fours and the fours become eights, until the whole group is stuck together and bouncing in unison.

Put your Worries Behind You

The children stand in a circle and simultaneously use imaginary pencils to sketch or write in the air a worry that's on their minds, then on a count of "1, 2, 3" cast the 'pencils' aside, snatch their own sketch or writing out of the air, scrumple it up and mime throwing it over their shoulders so it is behind them, out of the circle.

Shake, Rattle and Roll

The group stands in a circle. Hold a lightweight scarf high up in the air and suggest an action (e.g. shake your hands, roll your eyes, jump on the spot, etc) before dropping the scarf; the children do the action until the scarf touches the floor, then freeze.

Relaxation Holiday (relaxation)

Ask the class to sit or lie comfortably on the floor with enough distance between them so as not to distract each other. Invite them to close their eyes and then slowly read out the following:

Sit comfortably, start with a few slow, easy breaths and begin to relax...

and now let your mind create these sensations:

Imagine the colours of the sky in a beautiful sunset..

Imagine the sound of water flowing in a stream..

Imagine the smell of a bonfire on a crisp autumn day..

Imagine the feel of smooth, clean sheets..

Imagine the smell of a field of grass in the hot summer sun..

Imagine the stars and moon in the dark sky on a clear night..

Imagine the taste of a favourite food..

Imagine the sound of a beautiful song..

Imagine the wind blowing on your face..

Imagine floating on the still, shallow water of a peaceful lake...

Slow Motion

The children stand anywhere in the room and respond to the pace of your clapping by walking in time with it (e.g. slow claps mean walk slowly, fast claps mean jog, etc.)

Smile/Scowl Challenge

In pairs, one child scowls and one child smiles while staring at each other, until one of them can resist their partner's expression no longer and joins in (usually the smile triumphs).

Splat

Ask the group to make a circle. One person stands in the middle.

That person then throws an imaginary pie at one person in the circle.

That person must duck and the two people on either side throw an imaginary pie at each other and shout "SPLAT!".

If the first person doesn't duck, they are out. If they do duck in time, the last person to throw their pie on either side is out.

Continue until you are down to just two people left.

When there are only two people left begin THE DUEL: The two remaining players stand back to back in the middle of the circle. A category of words beginning with the same letter or a type of cereal is called out, such as 'weetabix'.

Each time the teacher calls out a cereal, the players take one step forward. When an object that is NOT a cereal is called out, they must throw their custard pies. The first to throw the pie is the winner.

Straight Face, Smile, Giggle

Sitting in a circle, one person starts by sending a neutral expression around the circle, then a smile, and then a giggle.

Stations

The class stands in a circle with one person in the centre, who calls out two children's names and then says "Change stations!" The two named children exchange places while the person in the centre tries to get into one of the empty places first. Whoever is left in the centre then calls out two more names and the game continues.

The Sun Shines on

Ask the group to arrange their chairs in a circle. With one person in the centre there should be no spare seats. The person in the centre will say a statement starting with 'The sun shines on...' For example they might say, 'The sun shines on everyone wearing blue.' Everyone in the group who is wearing blue then gets up and moves to another seat while the person in the middle will also try to find a seat to sit on.

Whoever is left without a seat has to stay in the centre of the circle and make the next statement.

The game can be continued for as long as you want or until the group runs out of fun statements.

Thunderstorm

The group stands in a circle. Start the first action for the child on your left to copy while you keep going, and so on around the circle until the action returns to you, then start the next action and so on:

gently rub palms together

tap two fingers on palm of one hand

clap hands

slap hands on thighs and stamp feet

clap hands

tap two fingers on palm of one hand

gently rub palms together

cross your arms to finish.

Three Ball / Beanbag Name game

Invite trainees to join you in a circle. Check that all name badges are clearly visible.

Give a ball/beanbag to three people evenly spaced around the circle.

One person starts by choosing another participant to throw to.

Before they throw they alter the other person by calling their name and looking at them before they throw them the ball/beanbag.

The catcher repeats the same process.

Gradually increase the number of ball/ beanbags in circulation.

Travellers' Tails [longer and for outside]

The class stands in a circle. Reward one child with the privilege of starting the game; to walk or run around the outside of the circle as a train/car/aircraft, etc.

Those who s/he touches on the shoulder leave the circle and follow, copying the action. When five others are following, call out "All change!" they all run to the nearest available space in the circle. Choose a different child to begin the next round; they must also choose a different method of transport for their travels.

What are you Doing?

The group stands in a circle. Choose one person to begin miming an action e.g. skiing. The person on their right asks 'What are you doing?'

The first person then says a different to the action they are miming e.g. riding a bike. The second person then starting miming 'ride a bike'

Repeat around the circle until it arrives back at the beginning.

Yoga Relaxation (relaxation)

The class sits in a circle. Invite everyone to rub their hands together fast until they are hot, then cup their hands over their eyes and take a few deep breaths. To let in the light gradually, spread the fingers and bring the hands down slowly over the cheeks.

Parachute games

Pass the Hooter /Recorder

Age Group: 6-9
Ideal Number: 15 – 25
Equipment Req'd: Parachute, hooter
Amount of Time: 10 mins

Reason for playing:
Reinforcing names learned

How to play:
- Everyone stands around the parachute, which is held at waist height.
- Someone starts by hooting a hooter/recorder and saying the name of somebody across the circle from them.
- The hooter/recorder is then placed on the parachute.
- The task of the group is to get the hooter to the named person by tipping, flicking, wafting the parachute.
- When it reaches that person they hoot the hooter and send it off to someone else.

Tent pole

Age Group: 6 – 11
Ideal Number: 15 – 25
Equipment Req'd: Parachute
Amount of Time: 10 mins

Reason for playing:
Fun

How to play:
- All crouch around the edge of the parachute, holding the edge with both hands.
- On the call "One, two, three, mushroom" players raise their arms, pulling the parachute above their heads – then take a step or two inwards, and pull the parachute down behind them, sitting on the edge to form a tent.
- One player is asked to stand in the centre and be the tent pole, supporting the canvas.
- They then call the name of another player, and the two attempt to swap places before the tent irretrievably collapses.
- Continue calling and changing places until all have had a turn as the tent pole.

Cool Frog

Age Group: 6 – 11
Ideal Number: 10 – 25
Equipment Req'd: Parachute
Amount of Time: 10 – 15 mins

Reason for playing:
Fun, activity

How to play:

- Spread the parachute out on the floor with everyone kneeling at the edge. (This is a giant lilypad).
- Choose someone to be 'grumpy frog' who sits in the middle of the lilipad.
- Everyone kneeling at the edge of the lilypad are the other frogs, who want to join the grumpy frog in the middle, but in order to not offend the rather grumpy frog, they must ask to be let on in a particular way.
- Start a rhythm (clicking fingers or clapping) and ask the questions "Hey, frog face can we have a bit of your space?"
- Grumpy frog will then say who will be allowed on the lilypad e.g. all those wearing red take one hop forwards.
- Hops can be forwards or backwards using any colour, theme or subject to select people.
- Repeat this process until everyone gets on to the centre of the lilypad.

Hot Dog

Age Group: 6 – 9
Ideal Number: 15 – 25
Equipment Req'd: Parachute
Amount of Time: 10 mins

Reason for playing:
Activity, variety

How to play:

- Somebody is needed to lead the game.
- All players crouch around the edge of the parachute.
- The leader goes around the circle naming each player either 'Hot Dog', 'Mustard' or 'Relish'.
- When one of these groups is called, all players with that name have to get up and run clockwise around the outside of the circle.
- When they are almost back to their places, the 'leader' calls "One, two, three, mushroom!" and everybody lifts the parachute so that the runners can go underneath.
- As they run under, the leader calls an instruction which they must quickly perform within their group, for example, 'Shake hands with each other' or 'bunny hop back to your places'.

Sharks

Age Group: 6 – 11
Ideal Number: 15 – 25
Equipment Req'd: Parachute
Amount of Time: 10 mins

Reason for playing:
Activity, fun

How to Play:

- All sit around the parachute with legs underneath it.
- One person is chosen to be the shark and goes underneath the parachute.
- Players make waves with the parachute while the shark is moving about.
- The shark chooses a victim by pulling their legs.
- The victim has to give a blood-curdling scream and goes underneath the parachute to replace the shark.
- You can have several sharks.

Mushroom

Age Group: 6 – 11
Ideal Number: 15 – 25
Equipment Req'd: Parachute
Amount of Time: 10 mins

Reason for playing:
Activity, variety, fun

How to Play:

- To begin with everyone is kneeling around the parachute holding it on.
- Someone shouts something like "Carrots, peas, brussel sprouts" and then the magic word "Mushrooms".
- Everyone then stands up holding the parachute above their heads and takes two steps forward, thereby creating a beautiful mushroom shape with the parachute.

Variations:

1. Make a mushroom

- Allocate players numbers and get them to run underneath the parachute when their number is called.
- Could call more than one or even all numbers at the same time.
- Could use vegetable or fruit names instead, and have a cry of "Vegetable Cart!" where everyone runs at the same time.

2. Make a mushroom

- Players put the parachute over their heads and sit down inside, on the edge of it.
- Can then play circle games inside it.

3. Make a mushroom

- Everyone lets go at exactly the same time.
- If there isn't any wind, the chute will retain it's perfect mushroom shape and rise straight up into the air.
- Indoors it may go up to the ceiling.
- To get this right, it's best for someone to shout "1, 2, 3, go!", or words to that effect, immediately after the "mushroom" instruction.
- For everyone to let go at exactly the right instant will require practice and consideration.

Colour Kaleidoscope

The whole class stands holding the parachute. Everyone is given the name of a colour (up to four colours in total).

When the caller calls out a colour name, the class holds the parachute aloft and those with that name change places beneath it.

Reward good behaviour by upping the anti: call two colours together, or "kaleidoscope!", at which everyone changes place while the parachute floats overhead, anchored only by the caller.

Washing Machine

Reward two children for good behaviour by inviting them to sit back-to-back, cross-legged, with their hands on their heads in the middle of the parachute. The others slowly walk around them, wrapping them up as they go.

When the parachute reaches the two children's elbows, the class stands still and on a count of 3 tugs the parachute.

The two children will spin around like laundry in a washing machine as the parachute untwists beneath them.

Cat and Mouse

Age Group: 6 – 11
Ideal Number: 10 – 25
Equipment Req'd: Parachute
Amount of Time: 10 mins

Reason for playing:
Fun

How to Play:
- Players stand in a circle holding the parachute, around waist height.
- Choose one or more players to be the 'cats'.
- Cats are on top of the chute.
- Mice go underneath the chute.
- Cats attempt to catch the mice.
- Other players hold the parachute and make waves to conceal the mice.
- Replace the mice when they have been caught.
- Change cats frequently so that everyone has a go.

Special Notes
When very young children are playing, keep the parachute quite low.

Thinking about offering parents a parenting course? Contact Family Links and take a look at *The Parenting Puzzle* book and accompanying DVD and Audio CD:

familylinks.org.uk

Find the Classroom Handbooks, games, DVDs and more in our website shop at

centreforemotionalhealth.org.uk

Book a *Developing Emotional Resilience* workshop for your school now!

centreforemotionalhealth.org.uk

Recommended background reading

The following are just a few titles selected from the wide range of books available on subjects such as child development, child psychology, neuroscience and the building of self-esteem, all of which support an emotionally literate approach to working with – and understanding the feelings and behaviour of – children.

- *Child Development from Birth to Eight: a practical focus* — Lindon, J. — NCB
- *Hearing the Truth: the importance of listening to children who disclose* — NCH Action for Children
- *Promoting Positive Behaviour* — O'Brien, T. — David Fulton Publishers
- *Dorothy Rowe's Guide to Life* — Rowe, D. — Constable
- *On Personal Power: Inner Strength & its Revolutionary Impact* — Rogers, C. — HarperCollins
- *How to Understand the Secret language of Children* — Shapiro, L. — Simon & Schuster
- *Life and How to Survive it* — Skinner, R. & Cleese, J. — Methuen
- *Achieving Emotional Literacy* — Steiner, C. — Bloomsbury
- *Blame my Brain* — Morgan, N. — Walker Books
- *Difficult Conversations: how to discuss what matters most* — Stone, D. et al — Penguin Books

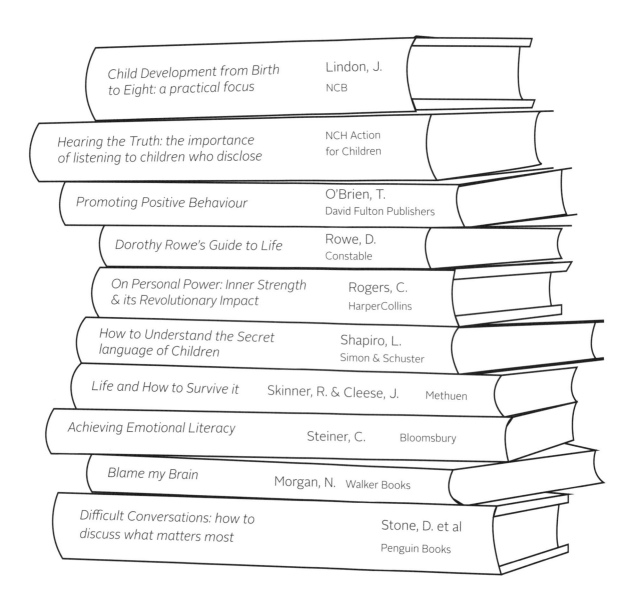

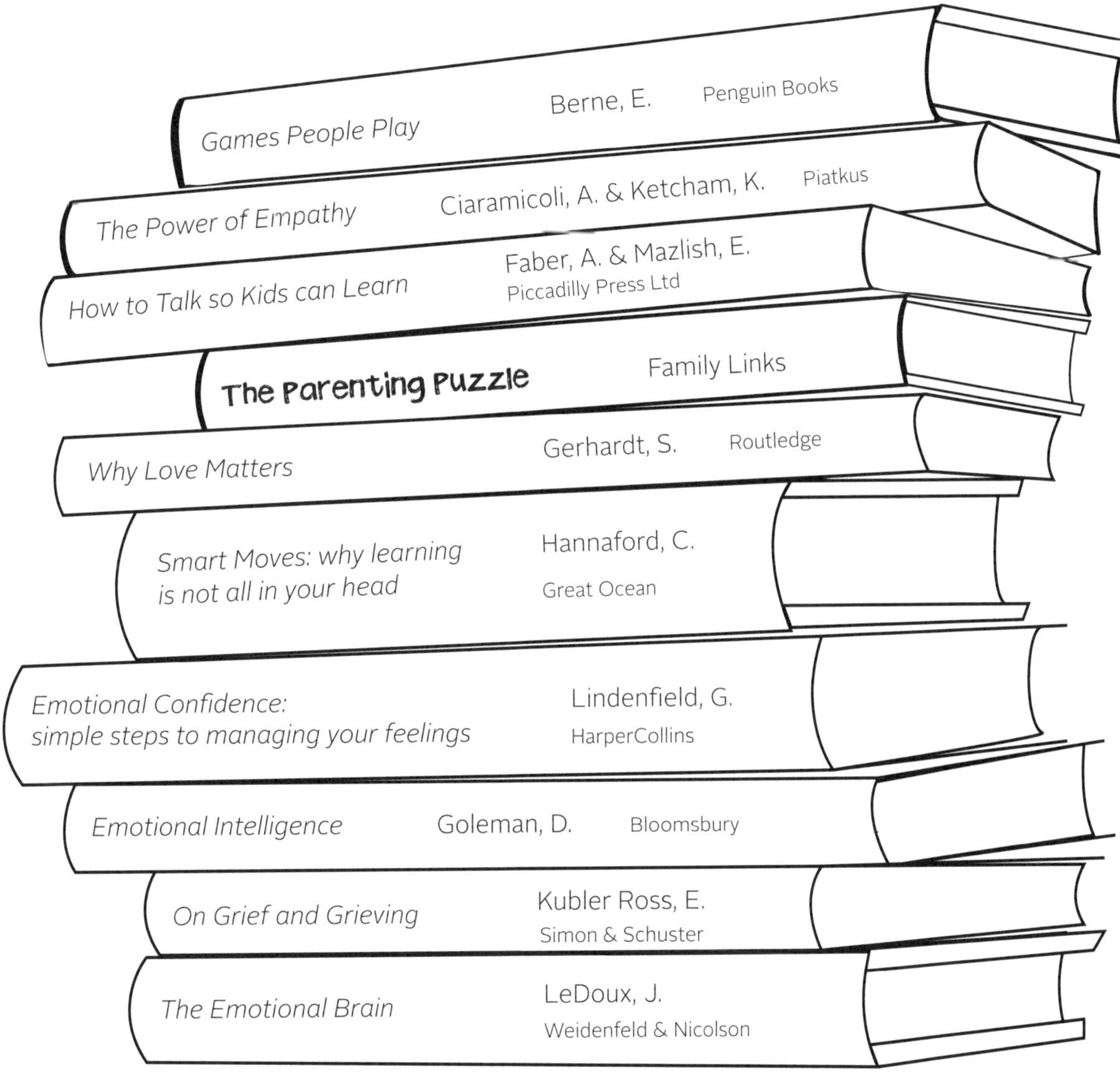
Games People Play
Berne, E.
Penguin Books
The Power of Empathy
Ciaramicoli, A. & Ketcham, K.
Piatkus
How to Talk so Kids can Learn
Faber, A. & Mazlish, E.
Piccadilly Press Ltd
The Parenting Puzzle
Family Links
Why Love Matters
Gerhardt, S.
Routledge
Smart Moves: why learning is not all in your head
Hannaford, C.
Great Ocean
Emotional Confidence: simple steps to managing your feelings
Lindenfield, G.
HarperCollins
Emotional Intelligence
Goleman, D.
Bloomsbury
On Grief and Grieving
Kubler Ross, E.
Simon & Schuster
The Emotional Brain
LeDoux, J.
Weidenfeld & Nicolson

We'd like to thank...

Annette Mountford

Founder and Patron, for her whole community vision for emotional health and wellbeing

Gail Allan, Sarah Darton, Claire Woodroffe, Rowen Smith and The Family Links team

for bringing the Nurturing Programme to life in schools and universities

Steph McCullough, Louise Cobb and Katie Whiteley

for their wisdom and advice on this edition.

Bea Stevenson

for managing the updates and additions in this second edition

Blackbird Academy Trust

All of the staff and children at the Blackbird Academy Trust for their support

index

Extra notes